The Book Industry in Transition

An Economic Study of Book Distribution and Marketing

by Benjamin M. Compaine

Knowledge Industry Publications, Inc.
White Plains, New York

Communications Library

THE BOOK INDUSTRY IN TRANSITION: An Economic
Analysis of Book Distribution and Marketing

by Benjamin M. Compaine

Library of Congress Cataloging in Publication Data

Compaine, Benjamin M.
  The book industry in transition.

  Bibliography: p.
  Includes index.
  1. Book industries and trade -- United States.
I. Title.
Z471.C66   658.8'09'0705730973   78-7527
ISBN 0-914236-16-4

Printed in the United States of America

TABLE OF CONTENTS

LIST OF TABLES AND CHARTS

This one is for Mom and Dad, who did just
about everything right.

PREFACE

This volume is one in a series of market analyses prepared by Knowledge Industry Publications, Inc., publishers of newsletters, library monographs and studies of communications-based companies. It is our feeling that there is a vacuum in that aspect of the business literature which deals with the dynamics of specific major industries, such as newspaper, magazine, music or book publishing.

The Book Industry in Transition: An Economic Analysis of Book Distribution and Marketing is meant to be a detailed description of how general books get to various markets, how the economics of this distribution work, what the strengths and weaknesses of the current practices are, what changes are affecting the book industry, and what may be the future directions of the industry. The book is drawn from the well-received market research that K.I.P. has undertaken for its industry clients.

The volume, however, has been written in non-technical language: it should be as readable by the layman or student as by the industry insider. It has attempted to avoid much of the jargon that those who are part of this industry (and most others) develop as sort of shorthand for meeting among themselves.

It is our desire that readers will find this book and others in the Communications Library valuable reference works.

Many people gave generously of their time and various organizations have given us permission to reprint or otherwise make use of data they have collected. Without their assistance this report could not have been assembled. In no particular priority, the author and Knowledge Industry Publications, Inc. wish to thank R.R. Bowker Co. and *Publisher's Weekly* for reprint rights to certain statistical data, as well as John Dessauer, the Book Industry Study Group, and the Association of American Publishers, all of whom are engaged in a successful struggle to bring some order into this sphere for the book publishing industry. I also appreciate the help of numerous publishers, wholesalers, retail booksellers and others involved in the book trade for information, ideas, and guidance.

Benjamin M. Compaine
Director, Communications Library
March 1978

I

Introduction

This report was written 47 years ago under a different name. It probably could have been written with few differences 100 years ago. The book industry is running hard and expending much energy, but economically it's on a treadmill — unable to generate much forward momentum except for what is provided by the American economy. As it moves forward, so does the book industry. But any progress is independent of the efforts on the treadmill.

What all this means is that in many ways, the problems, complaints, and needs of book publishers and sellers today are much as they were in 1931 when O.H. Cheney conducted an "Economic Survey of the Book Industry." In that landmark work, Cheney found:[1]

- Management and control methods were generally inadequate, particularly in the publishing and distribution branches.

- Hazards and wastes were unnecessarily high throughout the industry.

- No entirely new distribution system was then possible, but the existing machinery, "under present conditions," could not handle a reasonable volume profitably.

- The educational process which creates new readers was weak at a number of danger points.

[1] O.H. Cheney, *Economic Survey of the Book Industry* 1930-1931 (New York: R.R. Bowker Co., 1931), p. 9.

- The methods for promoting reading and book buying were inadequately organized and planned.

Much of this is still true today, to varying degrees. Book distribution is still a mess — but there are signs that mechanisms are developing for real improvement. There is still much waste and a lack of modern control procedures, but new elements in the industry indicate progress here, too. There has been little success in educating the general public in the benefits of reading, although increased widespread education has had an indirect effect. But any study of book buyers' motivation and behavior is still nonexistent, and aggressive promotion has developed on a small scale only in the past half dozen years.

This study is not an attempt to replicate Cheney's efforts, though it does provide contemporary evidence supporting much of his research. As an example, Cheney's sentiments about the book publishing and selling industry are maintained: "Those who take masochistic pleasure in calling the book industry 'thirty years behind the times' will get no thrill out of this report," he wrote in 1931.[2] The same holds true in 1978. Although it is true, for example, that many other industries are able to use far-flung distribution networks to push through a volume of goods far greater than the book industry could ever dream of handling, these are different industries with their own unique problems.

The book industry has been considered backward, perhaps because it is relatively small. In dollar terms, the total combined value of publishers' receipts in 1976, $4.2 billion, would place it only 41st on *Fortune*'s list of *individual* industrial firms, just ahead of Monsanto, just behind Beatrice Foods, Xerox, and Firestone Tire and Rubber Co. The publishing industry's importance, however, goes beyond its financial position, because books have always been bought and used by the most educated and wealthy members of society, creating prestige and influence far in excess of its raw size.

As manufacturing industries go then, book publishing is not a mass industry. Whereas "small" magazines may sell 500,000 copies of an issue each month, a hardcover book can reach the bestseller

---

[2] Cheney, p. 4.

list with sales of 40,000 over many months, and it is the rare book indeed that sells over 100,000 copies. Even the so-called mass market paperback books produce barely a handful that sell a million copies in their lifetimes. Moreover, the proliferation of new titles — there were 2067 new works of fiction alone in 1976, almost 27,000 new works in all categories — makes the volume of sales for any given title that much lower. Many paperback books are actually approaching the transience of a monthly magazine, lasting as little as two weeks on the newsstand and drugstore racks before they must be moved to make way for the next wave. A study performed several years ago measuring the length of time the average book remained on the *New York Times* bestseller list found that the stay shrank from 18.8 weeks (for a 1953-1956 period) to 15.7 weeks (1963-1966), a decrease of 16% in a decade.

Nonetheless, although the proliferation of books may be a problem from a business standpoint, sociologists use this phenomenon to support their contention that U.S. society is not becoming more homogeneous as a result of the mass media but, to the contrary, is showing ever greater diversity of interest.

THE STUDY AT HAND

The purpose of this project was to examine the current state of the distribution and marketing of general books. General books includes categories commonly referred to by those in the book business as "trade" (hardcover or paperback, adult and juvenile), mass market paperback books, university press, professional, and religious books. (Definitions of these terms are found in Chapter II.)

The impetus for a project of this scope at this time came from the frequently voiced comments of those in the industry that distribution is still a mess — though not many had concrete yet practical ideas for a change. One of the industry's foremost analysts, John Dessauer, has recommended industry sponsored "consolidation warehouses" around the country to speed the flow of orders from booksellers. The idea does not seem to have created much enthusiasm, for, among other reasons, it depends on industry-wide consent and implementation.

To speak of "the" industry is substantively naive. There are several industries: large companies with divisions publishing everything from Bibles to mass market paperbacks to textbooks; small trade-only publishers; publishing companies owned by large publicly held conglomerates; small "mom and pop" booksellers; large bookstore chains owned by retailing giants; national jobbers; librarians; local independent distributors; hardcover reprinters. The self-interests of each of these groups are not congruent and at points may be diametrically opposed. Trade associations of publishers, booksellers, and distributors try to provide some coordination, but they can go only as far as the uncommon interests of their membership allow. The United States also has strict antitrust laws that make any concerted industry efforts subject to close scrutiny.

So the conscious outcome of this project, given this industry environment, has been first, to assemble an analysis of the general status of the book industry, its recent historical trends, and the direction the industry appears to be taking; second, to present a cogent description of the way general books are being marketed and distributed; third, to share the techniques, innovations, and experiments that various organizations have undertaken or are presently trying, in the hope that each firm can build on what others have done; fourth, to provide an outsider's evaluation of which tools have been most useful, and which hold the most promise for making lasting improvements; and lastly, from this same perspective, to provide a sense of direction about how some of the most stubborn underlying problems can be remedied without major upheavals or clarion calls for massive industry-wide consortia. This last point is most crucial, for there is much that can be improved in book distribution merely by appealing to the selfish interests of individual companies in the industry. Bantam Books, an outstanding example, has already recognized much of this and is using its weight to help impose change on the industry. But most other firms must still undergo a process of self-discovery and careful analysis, after which they should reach the same conclusions.

THE MAJOR PROBLEMS

● The distribution network for selling books remains cumbersome and inefficient. A strong structure of wholesaler intermediaries such as exists in most other consumer industries selling small-ticket durable products has never developed in the book industry. This is aggravated by the phenomenal number of separate titles that an individual customer might want access to at a given moment. Publishers are caught in a Catch-22: To encourage booksellers to take countless untried products (each new title), they allow them to return books that they have bought. This procedure means that a publisher does not know how many copies he has really sold, often months after books were bought by booksellers. Also, it discourages booksellers from having the clearance sales of most other retail trades.

• The economics and structure of publishing preclude spending a substantial amount of money to promote any given title. Each new book is unique and must sell on its own (with a few exceptions for best-selling authors or movie hit tie-ins), but cannot be promoted with the gusto of a new brand of soap. Moreover, there is hardly any brand loyalty to a publisher: One may buy cars from Ford, but not books from Farrar, Straus & Giroux.

• There has been little tradition of hard-nosed business practices in publishing house management or in bookstore proprietorship.

• There remains a paucity of retail outlets for books, a vacuum that has not and cannot be completely filled by book clubs or mail order.

• In the view of a large number of people, too many books are being published — though as we shall see, this assumption bears careful analysis.

PREMISES FOR THE STUDY

After some preliminary surveying of the industry, the project proceeded under the following set of hypotheses:

• Distribution of so many products to so many individuals will always be a major problem, but it can be streamlined without a major change in existing structures.

• Access to books has become increasingly easier and will continue to do so, but is limited by the narrow segment of the population that buys books. If the industry can broaden the range of people interested in books, outlets will expand accordingly.

• Book publishers and sellers are moving to more professional management and decision-making techniques based on business factors, as well as on the traditional editorial impulses.

• Such business-related policies will result in fewer titles being published, but those eliminated will be primarily marginal works or duplicates of similar works of other publishers. Quality material will still find its way into print – as a justifiable business decision.

• New publishing formats will help keep the price of books affordable.

In retrospect, these hypotheses have been largely though not completely substantiated. (See Chapter XIII). But in any case they were most useful in providing a focus for the project.

One of the major limitations in this undertaking was the lack of reliable statistical data from many branches of the industry. Although the Association of American Publishers (AAP) has vastly improved its information-gathering capability in recent years, the changing of categories as well as improved reporting often make comparison with earlier periods impractical. This has forced greater reliance on estimates, but has also left unnecessary gaps. The American Booksellers Association (ABA) was generous in its sharing of data, but it is way behind most trade associations in collecting information on its membership. This is indicative of the unsystematic approach of the booksellers for many years, an approach that only now appears to be changing direction.

Fundamentally, the study has assumed that most of the change in distribution and marketing practices has to come from individual publishers, booksellers, and wholesalers, with some informational coordination and impetus from the trade associations. Although the intent of this study has not been to lay down a blueprint for action, its general findings and conclusions are cast in the framework of this modest assumption. No radical remedies are forthcoming, merely a suggestion of "a willingness to think and to work; courage to face facts and to experiment."[3]

---

[3]Cheney, p. 16.

II

Structure of the Industry

Book publishing is a relatively diffuse industry, labor intensive, characterized by easy entry. With few exceptions, printing is contracted out, and distribution for small publishers is often handled by a larger house. Some publishers become specialists in certain types of books: sex, science fiction, romance, crafts, art; others are regionally oriented.

STRUCTURE OF BOOK PUBLISHING

The book industry is divided into divisions, each of which is defined by the industry's current trade association (there have been a number of predecessors), the Association of American Publishers (AAP). Publishers are referred to in the industry as "houses," e.g., a trade house or a mass market house. Frequently, a publisher may be several "houses," combining different areas of publishing into separate divisions under a single corporate ownership.

The major divisions of the industry are:

● Trade books — marketed to the general consumer and sold primarily through bookstores and to libraries. Traditionally they have been hardcover, but there is a growing percentage of quality or trade paperback books. Trade books include both adult and juvenile titles and may touch on any subject, from fiction to music.

● Religious books — primarily Bibles and prayer books, but also other works of specific religious content, such as theological treatises. When a religious book publisher produces a title of wider interest, such as race relations or social problems, it would be classified as a trade or textbook, as indicated by its content and target audience. Religious books are distributed largely through specialized religious bookstores, though some titles are sold more widely.

- Mass market paperbacks — sold predominantly through newsstands, drugstores, chain retail stores, as well as an increasing number of general and paperback bookstores. Many are original titles, whereas others are reprints of titles that were originally published in hardcover. In addition to relying on a somewhat different mode of distribution than trade paperbacks, mass market paperbacks are usually printed on less costly paper, may have flashier covers, and are usually a standard 4¼ x 7 inch size.

- Professional books — divided into medical, technical and scientific, and business and other professional categories. They are directed at people in these occupations and are specifically related to the reader's work. Although professional books may be used in educational programs, this is considered to be a secondary market for these books.

- Mail order publications — titles created to be marketed by direct mail to the consumer. The books may be one-shot, but are frequently part of a continuing series related to a particular topic. Once the buyer agrees to buy one book, the publisher sends additional volumes automatically unless the customer sends the book back or terminates the agreement. Unlike book clubs, however, there is no commitment to buy any minimum number.

- Book clubs — really just channels of distribution for books originally published by others. Some do arrange for the printing of their own editions, however, and distribute them to their club members. Book clubs are further divided into consumer and professional clubs, the former including general interest clubs such as Book-of-the-Month, and special interest clubs, such as Outdoor Life Book Club.

- University press — characterized by their originating

source: nonprofit adjuncts to universities, museums, or research institutions. Though often similar in subject and distribution to trade or professional books, titles tend to concentrate on scholarly or regional topics.

• Elementary and secondary textbooks (el-hi textbooks) — hard or soft cover, workbooks, manuals, and maps intended for classroom use. Unlike trade books, they usually contain chapter summaries, questions, and projects. They are sold in bulk to school districts and in some states as part of state-wide standardized curricula.

• College textbooks — hard or soft cover. The category embraces many audiovisual items, all used in higher education (beyond high school). Government, industry, and libraries are among the secondary markets. Frequently there is little difference between a college textbook and a trade book, with publishers selling the same book to each market. The area that constitutes the bulk of the book's sales determines its category.

• Standardized tests — published to provide general measures of intelligence, aptitude, achievement, ability and the like in schools, colleges, and industry.

• Subscription reference books — primarily sets of encyclopedias sold through the mail or door-to-door, with a sizable market in libraries. Dictionaries, atlases, and other such publications originated by these publishers are included in this category.

It should be clear that, for the most part, publishing divisions are determined by methods of distribution: Books sold through general bookstores are trade, those to schools are el-hi, those to college students are college texts, etc.

To be sure, there is much overlap. In fact, the industry is becoming increasingly aware that the multiplicity of markets is resulting in the blurring of the older distinctions.

Mass market paperbacks are being used in ever greater numbers as part of school and college courses and are being sold through trade channels. Many trade books, hardcover and paperback are used in colleges and are being purchased by libraries. Mail order books are available through bookstores. Hence, AAP uses the concept of "predominance" in deciding in which slot to place a book. Though this is no doubt necessary to create a semblance of statistical order, it tends to put up barriers against expanding markets through creative distribution and promotion. Nonetheless, there is an increasing number of publishers who are breaking out of the traditional channels in an effort to sell books wherever they can find an audience for their titles.

INDUSTRY MARKETS

Books are sold to their ultimate users through several marketing channels:

● Retail stores – those that buy from others for resale to the final buyer or consumer. These include bookstores, book departments in department or chain stores (such as Gimbel's or K-Mart), supermarkets, drugstores, newsstands, museums, hobby shops, camera stores, art stores, medical suppliers, as well as stores that sell religious supplies, stationery, and gifts. In the industry pecking order, those outlets that traditionally have handled books for the general consumer are known as trade outlets, whereas the newer sellers, such as chain stores and supermarkets, are referred to as mass market outlets.

● College stores – the principal channel for college textbooks and other trade books used as part of course work. Many, however, also carry a line of books for discretionary purchases on the part of students and faculty. In many small communities with a college or university, they attract outside purchasers as well.

● Direct to consumer – transactions involving mail order, book clubs, and door-to-door sales to individuals.

● Libraries – including public, university, and private research libraries. El-hi school library sales are classified in the next category.

● Schools and institutions — comprising school system class-rooms, libraries, school stores, and any other institution that is public or private and includes kindergarten through grade 12.

● Miscellaneous markets — industry and government, premiums for businesses, foundations, and research institutions.

INTERMEDIARIES

In most industries, the channel of distribution to the retailer includes a middleman, called a jobber or whoesaler, who stocks the goods of many manufacturers and sells them locally, regionally, and occasionally nationally to retailers. Large retailers, such as major chain stores, act as their own wholesaler, ordering direct from all or most of the manufacturers whose products they carry. Book publishers have tended to place less emphasis than most other consumer industries on the intermediaries, selling directly to even the smallest of retailers. As this phenomenon is dealt with in more detail later, suffice it at this point to recognize that there are two — or more accurately two and a half — types of intermediate channels available to book publishers and retailers:

● Wholesalers/jobbers. These practically synonymous terms refer to those who perform the function of carrying an inventory of trade, professional, and mass market paperback books. Those who sell on a national or regional basis, relying on common carriers to ship their orders, are most frequently labeled jobbers. More local operations, generally supplying clients from their own trucks, are wholesalers, for those who cling to these distinctions.

● A subcategory of jobber is the small band (though not necessarily small in size) who specialize in fulfilling orders from the 30,000 libraries (other than school libraries) in the United States.

● Independent distributors (IDs). These are a type of whole-saler who are locally oriented. They originally were distributors of magazines, but most now also handle mass market paperback books and send them along to their newsstand, supermarket, stationery, and drugstore customers along with *Time* and *Playboy* magazines. Most publishers work through a national distributor who handles the paperwork involved in seeing that the IDs are sent new books and reorders; processes returns; but never physically takes possession of the publisher's books.

DISTRIBUTION OF PUBLISHING REVENUES

Half the firms in the publishing industry have four or fewer employees and account for only 1.9% of total industry receipts. At the other extreme, according to 1972 Census of Manufactures totals, the ten largest publishers accounted for nearly 23% of industry receipts. Table II-1 gives the distributions by size. In general, smaller firms are accounting for a decreasing amount of business and the largest firms are gaining market share. Still in comparison to other industries, book publishing is not highly concentrated. Periodicals, meat-packing plants, photographic equipment, and bakeries are among those industries with greater concentration; newspapers are less so.

Few of the industry's members can be called giants in the context of the American economy. McGraw-Hill had total sales in 1976 of $596 million, but less than half of these could be attributed specifically to book publishing. Time Inc., Times Mirror, and Macmillan are other large publishers on he *Fortune*

TABLE II-1:   Book Publishers by Size, 1972

Number of Employees	Number of Firms	% of Industry Receipts
1-4	604	1.9%
5-9	160	2.0
10-49	259	9.3
50-249	126	22.3
250-999	46	41.5
1,000 or more	10	22.9
	1,205	100.0

1972 Total Receipts — $2,856.8 (million)

SOURCE: U.S. Department of Commerce, 1972 Census of Manufactures.
NB: Totals may not add because of rounding.

500 list, but none had total book sales of more than $250 million. Table II-2 estimates the dozen largest book publishing firms by revenue.

TABLE II-2: Twelve Largest Book Publishing Companies, 1976

	Company	1976 Book & Book Related Revenues (in millions)
1.	McGraw-Hill	$255.7
2.	Grolier	246.9
3.	Doubleday[1]	239.8
4.	Harcourt Brace Jovanovich	225.3
5.	CBS Publishing[1]	220.8
6.	Prentice-Hall	209.6
7.	Time Inc.	192.0
8.	Macmillan	187.2
9.	Scott, Foresman	168.6
10.	Times Mirror	162.1
11.	Encyclopaedia Brittanica[2]	160.0
12.	Reader's Digest[2]	100.0

[1] In fiscal 1977, Doubleday had revenues of $335 million, reflecting the acquisition of Dell Publishing Co. In 1977, CBS had publishing revenues of $397 million, reflecting the acquisition of Fawcett (which is a book and magazine publisher). Hence, Doubleday and CBS would rank one and two as of 1977.

[2] Estimates. The acquisition of Lippincott by Harper & Row would make the consolidated company 12th in size with $141.2 million sales.

SOURCE: Corporate reports, except where noted.

GEOGRAPHIC DISTRIBUTION

The publishing business is concentrated largely on the East Coast, with New York alone accounting for almost a third of all publishing firms and most of the largest ones. Table II-3 compares the distribution of publishing companies in 1967 and 1972, showing that New York publishers actually increased slightly their proportion of total industry value of shipments despite small losses in the percentage of establishments and employees. Outside

TABLE II-3: Geographic Distribution of Book Publishers

	% of Establishments		% of Employees		% of Value Of Shipments	
	1972	1967	1972	1967	1972	1967
New England	8	7	7	6	7	8
Middle Atlantic	39	42	49	49	56	58
New York	31	34	40	42	49	48
E. North Central	16	20	22	28	24	26
W. North Central	5	5	8	6	6	3
S. Atlantic	9	7	3	2	1	1
E. South Central	2	3	2	3	1	1
W. South Central	3	3	1	*	1	*
Mountain	2	2	1	1	*	*
Pacific	14	10	8	3	4	2
Total	100	100	100	100	100	100

	No. of Establishments		No. of Employees (thousands)		Value of Shipments (millions)	
	1,205	1,022	57.1	52.0	$2,856.8	$2,134.8

*less than 1%.

SOURCE: U.S. Department of Commerce, *Census of Manufactures*, 1967 and 1972.

NB: Totals may not add because of rounding

of the Northeastern states, only the East North Central area — primarily Illinois — has a major publishing concentration. The rest of the country, then, is dotted with small, regional houses.

ECONOMIC STRUCTURE AND PROFITABILITY

Profitability in book publishing is largely a function of volume, as is true in any mass-production industry. Nonetheless, book publishing has the unique and unenviable characteristic of suffering many of the economic drawbacks of a job shop operation, despite the large aggregate number of books produced each year. This is especially true in the trade and professional book divisions where, unlike the education or mass market paperback markets, order quantities are generally small. A trade publisher, unlike a manufacturer of toothpaste or even magazines, ends up footing all the fixed, front-end costs for the product, but then finds the production run limited, resulting in a relatively high total cost per unit.

For example, a highly specialized professional book, with a sales potential of perhaps 2000 copies, incurs the same composition costs as a book of similar length that is expected to sell 10,000 copies. Editorial costs are not proportionally lower because of the fewer copies printed, and the burden for overhead must be allocated in an equitable manner — which again is not dependent on volume. Thus, the shorter run book incurs a higher fixed cost as a percentage of total costs than does a book with a larger printing. Table II-4 illustrates this analysis for three dif-

TABLE II-4: Book Publishing Costs at Alternative Levels of Production

	Number of Copies		
	2,000	5,000	10,000
Fixed and Semi-fixed			
Editorial and design	$ 3,500	$ 4,500	$ 6,000
Plant (composition and plates)	7,800	7,800	7,800
Overhead	5,000	5,500	5,500
Total fixed	16,300	17,800	19,300
Variable			
Printing, paper, binding	4,000	9,000	16,700
Promotion, warehousing, shipping	2,300	5,000	18,000
Royalty (based on 80% sold)[1] at $15 @ list price	3,600	9,000	12,000
Total variable cost	9,900	23,000	46,700
Total cost	$26,200	$40,800	$66,000
Fixed as % of total	62	43	29
Cost/book printed	$13.10	$8.16	$6.60

[1] Royalty at 15% of list on those sold.

ferent levels of production. This is not meant to be an actual profit analysis for a title, since it does not include any revenues, but it does recognize the reality that a publisher who expects to sell 10,000 copies may well plan on putting more money into editorial and design than he would in a title with a more limited potential.

For mass market paperback publishers, fixed costs per book become less consequential, as they deal in hundreds of thousands of copies and sometimes millions. Very high fixed costs are incurred on the occasional blockbuster titles that the hardcover houses auction off to reprinters for $500,000 or more. Although such auctions make big news, they are the exception. When Bantam bid $575,000 for *Jaws*, it calculated it needed sales of 1.6 million copies to break even, after which it would earn about $200,000 for each 600,000 books sold. Nonetheless, mass market paperback houses have their own cost problems to contend with. In order to reach a mass market, they must print far more copies than are actually sold. So, whereas trade publishers may get 20% of their shipments returned on a given title, some paperback publishers often contend with as much as a 60% return. Tables II-5 and II-6 provide operating ratios and pretax margins for several different types of publishers. Obviously, it becomes difficult to talk about the economic structure of the industry, since different divisions have markedly varying operating characteristics. In particular, there is the critical income from "other publishing" (book club and paperback rights primarily) that has spelled the difference between profit and loss for the trade publishers. In 1976, however, trade publishing wound up on the bottom rung in pretax profit averages. Profitability appears closely linked with overall volume, as subsequent chapters will show.

The economics of publishing may also be blamed for the glut of titles that are put out. Compared to the introduction cost for a new product in other manufacturing industries, the investment in a new book may be relatively low, especially if only the direct cost of composition and printing are considered. This would be the case in many small publishing houses where the owners may not consider their own time as a cost, whereas large houses may use a marginal costing calculation at times to justify a new title during a slack period. But the returns can be very great with a book that is a modest success. Using the assumptions of Table II-4, an 80% sale

TABLE II-5: Estimated Average Operating Ratios of Book Publishers, 1976

	Trade Books	Professional Books	Mass Market Paperback	El-Hi Text	College Text
Gross sales	117.4	114.9	154.9	103.5	117.7
Less returns, allowances	17.4	14.9	54.9	3.5	17.7
Net sales	100.0	100.0	100.0	100.0	100.0
Cost of sales					
Manufacturing	41.8	28.5	27.1	29.2	19.7
Royalties	14.1	9.5	27.5	6.1	15.1
Imports, exports, freight	1.7	2.7	5.8	—	1.2
Total cost of sales	57.6	40.7	60.4	35.2	36.0
Gross margin	42.4	59.3	39.6	64.8	64.0
Operating expenses					
Plant cost	—	—	—	5.7	6.7
Editorial	5.0	4.8	1.5	4.4	5.9
Production	1.8	1.8	1.0	1.5	1.5
Marketing	16.0	21.5	13.2	20.0	14.1
Fulfillment	9.9	5.7	6.1	8.3	6.5
General & administrative	11.3	12.2	8.7	12.7	11.1
Other	—	—	(0.2)	—	—
Total operating expenses	43.9	46.0	30.3	52.6	45.9
Net income before other publishing income	(1.5)	13.3	9.3	12.2	18.1
Other publishing income	8.9	1.2	—	1.0	0.4
Nonpublishing income	(0.3)	(0.1)	—	(0.4)	(0.3)
Net income before taxes	7.2	14.6	9.3	13.0	18.4
Taxes	3.9	7.2	—	6.9	8.6
Net income after taxes	3.2	7.4	—	6.1	9.7

Note: Totals may not add to 100.0 because of rounding.

SOURCE: Association of American Publishers, *Industry Statistics*, 1976.

TABLE II-6: Pretax Profit for Book Publishing Divisions, 1973 to 1976

	1973	1974	1975	1976
Adult hardbound	9.8%	6.5%	4.4%	1.7%
Adult paperbound	6.6	9.9	7.4	9.3
Juvenile	10.2	8.1	9.6	11.1
Professional	17.8	18.8	18.6	14.6
Book clubs	11.2	9.2	11.0	13.9
Mail order	8.0	3.0	9.8	23.2
El-Hi text	12.0	12.9	12.0	13.0
College text	14.2	16.6	18.9	18.4
Mass market	8.6	3.5	3.7	6.1

SOURCE: Association of American Publishers, *Industry Statistics,* annual.
Figures represent average for firms reporting to AAP in each division.
Industry-wide figures would likely be lower.

of 10,000 copies would gross about $69,600 for the publisher
(based on a receipt of 58% of list price). This would return a small
profit of $3600. Should the book ultimately sell 40,000 copies of
45,000 in subsequent printings, the publisher could earn almost
$95,000 before taxes. (Table II-7).

TABLE II-7: Profit and Loss Statement For a Trade Book Selling
40,000 Copies

Revenue ($8.70 net x 40,000)		$348,000
Expenses		
Fixed		18,300
Variable:		
Manufacturing	75,000	
Promotion, warehousing, etc.	70,000	
Royalties	90,000	
	235,000	
Total expense		253,300
Net income (before taxes)		$ 94,700

This is the financial attraction of publishing, the one title in ten that "makes it big." (On the average, three in ten titles are marginally profitable, 30% break even, and the remainder lose money, though some publishers can better this showing.) Publishers invariably add that these are the few big money-makers that allow them the luxury of publishing other books or first novels that they believe are deserving but are destined to lose money. These economic factors also explain why publishers think about the longevity of a title, since books in many categories can continue selling for years (one reason why cookbooks proliferate). Mass market paperback publishers work from a base of much larger numbers and smaller absolute margins, but the proportional economic characteristic remains the same.

THE COST/PRICE SPIRAL

Publishers have been hit hard by rapid escalation in paper costs since 1972. During that time, the price of paper has increased over 70%, whereas labor, printing, and binding moved up as much as 20% in 1974 alone. These increases in production cost have an effect on the price of books and may play a role in determining the number of titles that will be published. The breakdown of what happens to the money a consumer puts out for a trade hardcover book is seen in Table II-8:

For a paperback publisher, paper cost alone is 55% to 60% of the manufacturing cost, since the paperbacks are printed in such

TABLE II-8:   Where the Book Dollar Goes

	Direct	Through Jobber
Revenue	100%	100%
Retailer	43	40
Jobber	—	6
Manufacturing	20	20
Royalty	15	15
Promotion, distribution	15	11
Total	93%	92%
Overhead, profit	7%	8%

large quantities. But for a trade hardcover book, paper accounts for 25% to 45% of the cost, with the extra binding cost making up the difference. Moreover, if a publisher finds that because of increased paper, manufacturing, and other overhead cost he must net an additional $.50 per book, the list price for the book goes up over $1.00. For example, for a $5.95 list novel, the publisher averages net revenus of about $3.40. With added cost, he must now get $3.90. At a net of 57% of list, the new list price would be $6.85. However, since the author gets a royalty of 15% of the *list* price, he gets an additional $.135 at the higher price and the publisher would get only $.365 in real marginal revenue. So the publisher must raise the list price all the way to $7.25 — a 22% increase to realize a 14% increase in net marginal revenue. Hence the rapid price escalation of books.

SUMMARY

Book publishers are divided into 11 different divisions, defined primarily by the marketing channel and intended audience for the book. Books are sold through retailers and direct to the consumer, but there is also a major institutional market of libraries and schools, government and industry. Although there are wholesale intermediaries, publishers and retailers have tended to conduct more business directly than economic sense would dictate.

Although book publishers are highly concentrated in the Northeast and in the New York City area there are nonetheless hundreds of publishers scattered throughout the country. Compared to many other manufacturing industries, publishing is not dominated by one or a small group of firms, with the ten largest units accounting for less than a half of all sales.

As with any manufacturing enterprise, volume is crucial in lowering per unit costs. But the unique nature of each separate book makes volume production difficult. Compared to magazine production, even most mass market paperback books are relatively short runs, with many hardcover editions having to absorb large amounts of fixed cost per unit. Retail prices of books have increased sharply because of massive rises in paper cost, as well as labor. By the time they are passed on to the consumer, these increases are multiplied by added margin and royalty effects.

III

Size and Growth Trends
of the Book Publishing Industry

SIZE

Book publishing is a relatively small industry. The value of industry sales for 1976 was estimated by the Association of American Publishers at $4.2 billion, up 8.7% from 1975. Sales of $4.2 billion in 1976 compares to receipts of $4.6 billion for the periodical publishing industry and sales of $11.2 billion for newspaper publishing and printing.[1] According to the U.S. Commerce Department, there were 1250 book publishing establishments in 1977, an increase of over 20% from ten years earlier. The book publishing industry accounts for 5.6% of personal comsumption expenditures for recreation and employs about 56,000 workers.

SALES GROWTH OF THE INDUSTRY

The book publishing industry as a whole has leveled off in recent years following a decade of heavy growth through the 1960s, although its gain in 1976 was strong. Table III-1 compares publishing receipts to the Gross National Product. The strong growth in book publishing can be partly traced to the huge increases in government funds for education and libraries. As seen

---

[1] Throughout this study, book publishing figures are those provided by the Association of American Publishers (AAP). Although these figures are adjusted following the compilations made every five years by the Commerce Department's Census of Manufactures, AAP totals generally exceed the Census figures because they include sales of audiovisual materials and university presses, which the Census does not include, but they exclude coloring books, some pamphlets, and Sunday School materials counted in the Census.

TABLE III-1: Book Industry Sales and GNP, Selected Years, 1958-1976

Year	Book Industry Sales (millions)	% change	GNP (billions)	% change
1958	$ 946.1	–	$ 447.3	–
1963	1685.7	78.2%	590.5	32.0%
1967	2320.0	37.6	793.9	34.4
1968	2594.0	11.8	864.2	8.8
1969	2763.1	6.5	930.3	7.6
1970	2924.3	5.8	977.1	5.0
1971	2921.4	(0.1)	1055.5	8.0
1972	3007.2	2.9	1155.2	9.4
1973	3197.6	6.3	1306.6	13.1
1974	3533.0	10.5	1413.2	8.2
1975	3810.0	7.8	1516.5	7.3
1976	4185.2	9.8	1691.6	11.5
1958-1976	–	342.4	–	278.2

SOURCE: Book sales: Association of American Publishers; GNP: U.S.
Department of Commerce.

in Table III-2, the largest proportional increases among publishing categories were in the new trade paperback classification and the "other" category, which includes remainder sales and audiovisual materials. Both increased over 2000%, albeit from small bases. As seen in Table III-3, among the more established categories, mass market paperbacks and college textbooks have shown the largest relative gains since 1963, followed closely by professional and trade hardcover books. The gain for hardcover came despite an accounting change in 1971 that moved many sales previously counted in this category to the new mail order category. Juvenile books showed the weakest gains, while book clubs, despite their proliferation in numbers, have increased only modestly in sales. (Here again, however, many sales previously made in this group were transferred to the mail order classification, resulting in an indeterminable drag on the sales total – note the drop between 1970 and 1971.)

Since 1963, there have been several considerable shifts in the percentage sales volume accounted for by various categories. As

TABLE III-2: Estimated Book Publishing Sales, Selected Years, 1958-1976 (millions of dollars)

	1958	1963	1967	1970	1971	1972	1973	1974	1975	1976	Increase 1958 to 1976
Trade	$121.2	$ 229.5	$ 353.0	$ 409.0	$ 422.7	$ 442.0	$ 460.1	$ 522.7	$ 549.2	$ 573.3	373.0%
Hardcover	61.6	108.5	156.0	214.0	242.0	251.5	264.8	308.2	313.4	331.0	437.3
Paperback	5.5	17.0	32.0	47.0	69.6	79.6	86.7	97.3	111.2	117.8	2,041.8
Juvenile	54.0	103.9	165.0	148.0	111.1	110.9	108.6	117.2	124.6	126.5	130.7
Religious	37.8	81.1	108.0	113.0	108.5	117.5	124.7	130.6	154.6	171.2	352.9
Bibles, Testaments, Hymnals and Prayerbooks	N/A	35.0	51.0	N/A	54.4	61.6	66.5	67.5	76.6	83.6	
Other religious	N/A	46.1	57.0	N/A	54.1	55.9	58.2	63.1	78.0	87.6	
Professional	94.7	165.6	237.0	297.0	353.0	381.0	405.4	466.3	501.2	559.0	490.3
Medical	N/A	24.1	38.0	57.0	52.4	57.0	60.8	71.7	83.4	195.2	
Business and other professional	N/A	72.2	94.0	115.0	178.3	192.2	206.2	236.3	242.3	266.8	
Technical, scientific	N/A	69.2	105.0	125.0	122.3	131.8	138.4	158.3	175.5	195.2	
Book clubs	100.2	143.4	180.0	248.0	229.5	240.5	262.4	283.6	303.4	343.1	242.4
Mail order	N/A	N/A	N/A	N/A	194.6	198.9	221.2	247.0	279.8	348.9	
Mass market paperbacks	54.1	87.4	130.0	199.0	228.8	252.8	285.9	293.6	339.6	415.4	667.8
University press	7.1	18.3	31.0	39.0	39.3	41.4	42.6	46.1	48.8	53.5	653.5
Elementary and secondary text	195.8	304.7	421.1	484.0	498.6	497.6	547.9	598.8	643.1	640.1	226.9
College text	83.8	160.2	286.7	360.4	379.1	375.3	392.2	453.4	530.6	564.0	573.0
Standardized tests	8.4	12.7	21.6	23.1	25.3	26.5	28.8	34.2	36.2	40.0	376.2
Subscription references	234.3	380.9	441.0	N/A	301.0	278.9	262.2	280.2	258.1	286.5	22.3
Other	8.6	102.0	110.0	139.0	141.0	154.8	164.2	176.0	164.9	190.2	2,111.6
Total	$946.1	$1,685.7	$2,320.0	$2,924.3	$2,921.4	$3,007.2	$3,197.3	$3,533.0	$3,810.0	$4,185.2	342.4

N/A: Not available or applicable.

NOTE: Beginning in 1972, the AAP changed its reporting categories, which previously paralleled those of the U.S. Census of Manufactures. As a result of this change, data from before 1971 are not always directly comparable to data in the same categories in later years. The principal differences between the categorization employed before 1971 and the current definitions are as follows:

1) Mail order publications (i.e., books created primarily for direct marketing by mail to the consumer), reported before 1972 under Adult Hardbound, Juvenile, and Book Club;

2) Certain Trade Books, such as dictionaries, gardening books, how-to-do-it books, plays, etc., previously classified within "Other" category now are included under Adult Hardbound;

3) Books on non-religious subjects by religious publishers, reported previously under "religious" regardless of subject matter, now included in Adult Trade or Juvenile;

4) Professional books were defined in 1972 as follows: "Technical and scientific books" include only those on the physical, biological and social sciences, and on technology, engineering, and the trades created primarily for practicing and research scientists, architects, technicians, mechanics, and teachers in these fields.

"Business and other professional books" are those for managers, accountants, and individuals in professions and trades not covered by technical and scientific books, such as lawyers and librarians. Loose-leaf services are not included.

"Medical books" are those designed for the practicing medical professions.

5) Other category includes only sheet sales, domestic and export (except those to prebinders), remainder sales, as well as sales of audiovisual and sundry other non-print products.

SOURCE: Association of American Publishers, *Industry Statistics*, annual.

TABLE III-3: Growth in Publishers' Receipts and Economic Indicators, Selected Years, 1967-1976 (Index: 1963=100)

	1967 Index	1971 Index	1972 Index	1973 Index	1974 Index	1975 Index	1976 Index
Sales of All Books	141.1	173.3	178.4	189.7	209.6	226.0	248.3
Trade Hardcover	143.8	223.0	231.8	244.0	284.0	288.8	305.1
Trade Paperback	188.2	409.6	468.2	570.0	572.4	654.1	692.9
Juvenile	158.8	106.9	106.7	104.5	112.8	119.9	121.8
Book Club	125.5	160.0	167.7	183.0	197.8	211.6	239.3
Mail Order[1]	—	—	—	—	—	—	—
Professional	143.1	213.2	230.0	244.8	281.6	302.7	337.6
Mass Market Paperback	148.7	261.8	289.2	327.1	335.9	388.6	475.3
Elementary & Secondary Texts	138.2	163.6	163.3	179.8	196.5	211.1	210.1
College Texts	179.0	236.6	234.3	244.8	283.0	331.2	352.1
GNP (current $)	134.0	178.7	195.6	221.3	239.3	256.8	286.4
Personal Consumption Expenditures	131.2	177.9	194.4	214.7	233.7	256.7	N/A

[1] Began as a separate category in 1971. Before that, sales were included in trade, book clubs, and juvenile book categories.

SOURCES: Book Receipts: Association of American Publishers; GNP and Personal Consumption Expenditures: U.S. Department of Commerce, Bureau of Economic Analysis.

TABLE III-4: Books Sold by Category as a Percentage of Total Publishers' Receipts, Selected Years, 1963-1976

	1963	1967	1971	1972	1973	1974	1975	1976
Trade Hardcover	6.4	6.6	8.3	8.4	8.3	8.7	8.2	7.9
Trade Paperback	1.0	1.3	2.4	2.6	2.7	2.8	2.9	2.8
Juvenile	6.2	6.9	3.8	3.7	3.4	3.3	3.3	3.0
Total Trade	13.6	14.8	14.5	14.7	14.4	14.8	14.4	13.7
Book Clubs	8.5	7.8	7.8	8.0	8.2	8.0	8.0	8.2
Professional	9.8	10.2	12.1	12.7	12.7	13.2	13.2	13.4
Mail Order	—	—	6.7	6.6	6.9	7.0	7.3	8.3
University Press	1.1	1.3	1.3	1.4	1.3	1.3	1.3	1.3
Mass Market Paperback	5.2	5.4	7.8	8.4	8.9	8.3	8.9	9.9
Religious	4.8	4.6	3.7	3.9	3.9	3.7	4.1	4.1
General Books % of Total Sales	43.0	44.1	53.9	55.9	56.3	56.3	57.2	58.7
College Text	9.5	12.0	13.0	12.5	12.3	12.8	13.9	13.5
Elementary and High School Text	18.1	17.7	17.1	16.5	17.1	16.9	16.9	15.1

SOURCE: Table III-2.

seen in Table III-4, trade hard and softcover books provided 7.4% of industry sales in 1963, but by 1976 these books combined to produce 10.7% of the industry total, but down from 11.5% in 1974. College text sales have become more important, whereas elementary and secondary text sales have become relatively less so. Mass market paperbacks, already a well-established commodity by 1963, almost doubled their industry share to 9.9% of total book sales.

Over the past 15 years, the book publishers have failed in expanding their share of the discretionary dollar expenditures of individuals and nonprofit institutions. Table III-5 compares sales of books and maps to several other sources of such expenditures, showing that of these, only expenditures on admission to motion pictures increased at a slower rate. In all, books and maps, accounting for 7.3% of recreational expenditures in 1960, reached as much as 7.9% in 1965 before retreating down to 5.8% in 1975. Comparing the index of book sales in Table III-3 with total personal consumption expenditures, using data that continue to 1975, indicates again that the momentum of the 1960s is still dissipating, with book sales now failing to keep pace with competition from other leisure industries.

GROWTH IN OUTPUT AND PRICES

The growth in dollar sales has been greater than the increase in the volume of books sold in recent years. Between 1963 and 1972, publishers' receipts for college textbook sales increased by 135% on a unit increase of 93%. In elementary textbook sales, the difference is even more dramatic, with only 16% greater unit sales resulting in 75% more revenue in the same period. Table III-6 compares the revenue and copies sold for general books, again showing a similar phenomenon. The gap between unit volume and dollar volume has doubtlessly widened further with the rapid price escalation since 1972.

Although inflation has affected all prices, Table III-7 indicates that book prices have escalated at a rate considerably greater than overall consumer prices. Hardcover prices, reversing a falling trend in 1972 and 1973, jumped significantly in 1974 and 1975,

TABLE III-5: Personal Consumption Expenditures for Recreation
[Index: 1960=100 (in millions of dollars)]

	1950	1955	1960	1965	1970	1975
Total Recreation Expenses	$11,147	$14,078	$17,855	$25,907	$40,999	$66,100
Index	62	79	100	145	230	370
Books and Maps	$ 674	$ 867	$ 1,139	$ 1,648	$ 2,356	$ 3,397
Index	59	76	100	145	207	298
Magazines, newspapers, sheet music	$ 1,495	$ 1,869	$ 2,164	$ 2,662	$ 3,900	$ 7,502
Index	69	86	100	123	180	347
Admissions to motion picture theaters	$ 1,376	$ 1,326	$ 956	$ 1,067	$ 1,521	$ 2,538
Index	144	139	100	112	159	265
Radio and TV receivers, records, musical instruments	$ 2,421	$ 2,869	$ 3,003	$ 5,041	$ 8,885	$14,576
Index	81	96	100	168	296	485
Spectator sports	$ 222	$ 230	$ 354	$ 668	$ 1,064	$ 1,572
Index	63	65	100	189	301	444
Book sales as % of total recreation expenditures	6.0%	6.2%	7.3%	7.9%	7.1%	5.8%

NOTE: Represents market value of purchase of goods and services by individuals and nonprofit institutions.

SOURCE: U.S. Department of Commerce, Bureau of Economic Analysis, *Survey of Current Business.*

TABLE III-6: Revenue and Copies Sold, General Books, 1963 and 1972

	1963	1972	% increase
Copies sold (est.) (million)	751	1042	38%
Publisher receipts (million)	$827	$1671	102%

SOURCE: *The Bowker Annual of Library and Book Trade Information, 1974.*

TABLE III-7: Average Prices of Books, Selected Years, 1953-1976 (Index: 1967=100)

	All Hardcover Books		Mass Market Paper		Consumer Price
	Price	Index	Price	Index	Index
1953	$ 4.13	49.0	N/A		80.1
1958	5.12	60.7	N/A		86.6
1962	5.29	62.8	$ .53	70.7	90.6
1967	8.43	100.0	.75	100.0	100.0
1970	11.66	138.3	.95	126.7	116.3
1971	13.25	157.1	1.01	134.1	121.3
1972	12.99	154.1	1.12	149.3	125.3
1973	12.20	144.7	1.17	156.0	133.1
1974	14.09	167.1	1.28	170.7	148.3
1975	16.19	192.0	1.46	194.6	161.2
1976	16.32	193.5	1.60	213.3	170.5

SOURCE: Book prices: *Publisher's Weekly.* Consumer Price Index: U.S. Bureau of Labor Statistics.

resulting in an overall increase since 1967 almost as great as that in the steadily climbing mass market paperback field. From another viewpoint, Table III-8 lists the percentage increase in several hardcover categories, plus trade paperbacks. Of these, only business books, the highest priced in 1965, did not exceed the percentage increase in consumer prices.

As with all of the previously seen indexes of growth in book publishing, the rate of increase in the number of book titles issued each year exploded in the 1960s and has subsided just as quickly

TABLE III-8: Changes in Average Book Prices in Selected Categories, 1965 and 1976

	Prices 1965	1976	Increases 1965-1976 (%)
Consumer Price Index	–	–	80.4
All hardcover books	$7.65	$16.32	113.3
Fiction	4.34	9.87	127.4
Juvenile	3.11	5.87	88.7
Sociology & economics	8.43	20.03	137.6
Literature	6.90	14.65	112.3
Poetry, drama	4.70	12.41	164.0
Biography	7.65	14.81	93.6
Business	9.68	16.22	67.6
Trade and higher priced paperback books	2.50	5.53	121.2

SOURCE: R.R. Bowker Co., *Publisher's Weekly.*

since then. Table III-9 traces the trend in the rate of change of new book titles since 1950. Between 1960 and 1965, the new title output (in all cases including new editions) skyrocketed an astounding 90.5%, for an average annual growth of 18.1%. The

TABLE III-9: Title Output, Selected Years, 1950-1976

	Total (incl. new editions)	Average Annual % Increase
1950	11,022	–
1955	12,589	2.8%
1960	15,012	3.8
1965	28,595	18.1
1970	36,071	5.2
1971	37,692	4.5
1972	38,053	0.1
1973	39,951	5.0
1974	40,849	2.2
1975	39,372	– 3.6
1976	35,141	–10.7

Total Increase in Annual Title Output
1950-1976 – 318.8

SOURCE: R.R. Bowker Co., *Publisher's Weekly.*

TABLE III-10:   Change in Volume of Book Output by Categories, 1965 to 1976.

	1965	1976	% change
Total title output (new book & new editions)	28,595	35,141	22.9
Subject areas with output at or above total % change			
Biography	685	1,714	150.2
Home economics	300	690	130.0
Sociology, economics	3,242	5,960	83.8
Agriculture	270	477	76.7
Sports, recreation	591	1,034	75.0
Medicine	1,218	2,128	74.7
General works	634	1,034	63.1
Law	436	698	60.1
Business	537	843	57.0
Art	971	1,369	41.0
Poetry, drama	994	1,307	31.5
Technology	1,153	1,489	29.1
Subject areas with output below total % change			
Philosophy, psychology	979	1,192	21.8
History	1,682	1,934	15.0
Fiction	3,241	3,458	6.7
Music	300	302	0.7
Religion	1,855	1,748	-5.8
Science	2,562	2,342	-8.6
Literature	1,686	1,405	-16.7
Language	527	409	-22.4
Juvenile	2,895	2,210	-23.7
Travel	883	499	-43.5

SOURCE: *Publisher's Weekly.*

momentum continued through the rest of the decade, adding over 30,000 new titles and 10,000 new editions in 1974 to almost 400,000 titles in print. Categories showing the greatest increase in the number of new titles compared to 1965 include biography (1714 in 1976, up 150%) and home economics (690 in 1976 up 130%). Among those categories with the greatest decline from their 1965 rate of introduction are travel (down 43%) and juvenile

TABLE III-11: Book Sales Compared to School Enrollment and Personal Consumption (1972 dollars)

	1968	1970	% change	1974	% change	1976	% change	% change 1968-1976
Elementary and High School Texts (million constant $)	538.7	529.5	-1.7	470.4	-11.2	478.4	1.7	-11.2
El-Hi enrollments (million)	45.0	48.7	8.2	46.5	-4.5	45.5	-2.2	1.1
College texts (million constant $)	383.1	394.3	2.9	389.5	-1.2	421.5	8.2	10.0
College and Higher Ed. enrollments (million)	7.5	8.6	14.7	10.2	18.6	11.2[1]	9.8	49.3
General books (million constant $)	1,362.0	1,427.8	4.8	1,708.8	19.7	1,836.1	7.4	34.8
Personal consumption expenditures (billion constant $)	634	669	5.6	759	13.5	814	7.2	28.4

[1] estimate

SOURCE: Book Sales: AAP.
School Enrollments: U.S. Bureau of the Census, *Current Population Reports.*
Personal Consumption Expenditures: U.S. Bureau of Economic Analysis.
Higher Education Enrollments: U.S. Center for Education Statistics, *Digest of Education Statistics.*

(down 24%). Nonetheless, as seen in Table III-10, most categories have seen some increase in the number of titles.[2]

Although the growth in the volume of book sales is tied to a multiplicity of factors, Table III-11 examines sales of elementary/secondary and college textbooks, as well as the sales of general books, measured in constant dollars, and compares them to two measures: real personal consumption expenditures and school enrollments. Not surprisingly, general book sales appear to roughly follow the trend in consumption expenditures; education sales are more a product of the school population. Unit sales figures indicate that publishers are selling fewer total books to the schools and to university students, although at higher per volume prices.

CONCLUSIONS ON GROWTH

In the 1958 to 1976 period, the overall book industry surpassed the growth rate of the economy, spurred by increases in volume and prices, as well as because of the impetus of expanding educational enrollments in the 1960s. However, most indexes agree that this era of rapid growth in educational and institutional sales of textbooks is over. Further growth in the industry will have to depend on the sales of general books: the adult hardcover, the trade paperback, as well as the mass market paperbacks and professional books. It is for this reason that an examination of the means of distribution of this classification of books is particularly crucial at this time.

---

[2] *Publisher's Weekly* estimates that certain categories of books may be underreported, especially textbooks and mass market paperbacks. Actual totals may be 3%-4% higher.

IV

A Study of Who Buys Books, Where and Why

MEASURES OF BOOK BUYING

Getting books to the educational and library markets has been less of a problem than getting books to the individual consumer. In the former case, customers are manageable in number and are readily identifiable. All are, by definition, book buyers. This is not the case with the general population. It has been estimated that as few as 2% of the adult population are book buyers, although a study conducted in 1963-64 found that in three major cities, 40% of adults questioned had purchased a book in the previous month.[1] (In addition, book club membership itself includes 6% of the adult population.)

In a benchmark effort to establish who and where are the readers of books, so that publishers and sellers could more accurately reach them, O.H. Cheney investigated a broad array of possible variables that might affect book-buying habits.[2] From his findings, Cheney constructed an index of potential book purchases by state and compared them to an index of actual sales of books, finding, not surprisingly, that states such as New York, California, Connecticut, and Massachusetts significantly exceeded their potential, whereas almost all other states fell short of their potential.

Subsequent surveys have confirmed that book buying is not spread evenly among the population, with the percentage of total book sales far exceeding the proportion of the national population

---

[1] Richard Brown, "Book Buying," *Publisher's Weekly*, May 5, 1964, pp. 16-19.

[2] O.H. Cheney, *Economic Survey of the Book Industry*, 1930-1931 (New York: R.R. Bowker Co., 1931).

TABLE IV-1: Bookstores, Population, and Income by States

	# of Bookstores (1973)	% of Total Bookstores	% of Adult Population (18 and over) (1973)	% of Adults over 25, College Graduates (1973)	Per Capita Income as % of U.S. per Capita (1973)
U.S.	12,091	100.0%	100.0%	100.0%	100.0%
New England	952	7.8	5.9	6.7	105.0
Maine	82	0.7	0.5	0.4	80.2
New Hampshire	88	0.7	0.4	0.4	93.1
Vermont	45	0.4	0.2	0.2	81.6
Massachusetts	415	3.4	2.8	3.4	106.4
Rhode Island	65	0.5	0.5	0.4	97.2
Connecticut	257	2.1	1.5	2.0	119.7
Middle Atlantic	1,956	16.2	19.2	19.7	110.6
New York	857	7.1	9.4	10.6	115.1
New York City	561	4.6	3.8[1]	–	–
Pennsylvania	707	5.8	6.1	5.0	99.5
New Jersey	392	3.2	3.7	4.1	117.1
E. North Central	2,485	20.5	19.5	17.4	106.8
Ohio	594	4.9	5.2	4.5	101.9
Indiana	442	3.6	2.5	2.0	99.8
Illinois	687	5.7	5.5	5.4	117.0
Michigan	478	4.0	4.2	3.7	110.6
Wisconsin	284	2.3	2.1	1.9	94.2
W. North Central	916	7.6	8.0	7.4	98.0
Minnesota	212	1.8	1.8	1.9	100.1
Iowa	153	1.3	1.4	1.2	99.0
Missouri	240	2.0	2.4	2.0	95.0
North Dakota	43	0.4	0.3	0.2	97.2
South Dakota	38	0.3	0.3	0.2	97.4
Nebraska	89	0.7	0.7	0.7	98.1
Kansas	141	1.2	1.1	1.2	102.8
South Atlantic	1,749	14.5	15.0	14.8	92.5
Delaware	40	0.3	0.3	0.3	112.5
Maryland	183	1.5	1.9	2.5	108.4
District of Columbia	110	0.9	0.4	0.6	137.6

Virginia	296	2.4	2.2	2.6	95.9
West Virginia	70	0.6	0.9	0.6	77.8
North Carolina	263	2.2	2.4	1.9	83.8
South Carolina	130	1.1	1.2	1.0	77.6
Georgia	200	1.6	2.2	1.8	86.3
Florida	457	3.8	3.6	3.5	94.5
E. South Central	685	5.7	6.2	4.5	77.4
Kentucky	197	1.6	1.6	1.0	80.7
Tennessee	250	2.1	1.9	1.4	80.2
Alabama	153	1.3	1.6	1.2	75.7
Mississippi	85	0.7	1.0	0.8	70.1
W. South Central	903	7.5	9.2	8.6	84.5
Arkansas	67	0.6	1.0	0.6	74.8
Oklahoma	131	1.1	1.3	1.2	85.2
Louisiana	157	1.3	1.6	1.4	77.8
Texas	548	4.5	5.3	5.4	88.2
Mountain	568	4.7	3.8	4.6	92.5
Montana	50	0.4	0.3	0.3	89.8
Idaho	47	0.4	0.3	0.3	87.9
Wyoming	25	0.2	0.2	0.2	97.9
Colorado	177	1.5	1.0	1.4	102.6
New Mexico	81	0.7	0.4	0.5	76.5
Arizona	124	1.0	0.8	1.0	91.6
Utah	47	0.4	0.4	0.6	81.4
Nevada	17	0.1	0.2	0.2	113.1
Pacific	1,877	15.5	13.1	16.2	108.2
Washington	233	1.9	1.7	2.0	101.4
Oregon	142	1.2	1.0	1.2	95.5
California	1,425	11.8	9.9	12.5	110.6
Alaska	25	0.2	0.1	0.2	114.1
Hawaii	52	0.4	0.4	0.5	108.0

[1] New York City population vs. total population, 1970.

SOURCES: Bookstores: R.R. Bowker Co.
Population: U.S. Bureau of the Census, *Current Population Reports.*
Income: U.S. Bureau of Economic Analysis, *Survey of Current Business.*

in the Northeastern and Pacific states, whereas the reverse is true in the rest of the country. Underbuying is most pronounced in the Southeastern states.

The major problem has been the inaccessibility of much of the population to books, because bookstores have been concentrated in high population density areas. In many cases, book clubs and mail order were the primary routes of books to less urbanized areas that could not support bookstores. Today, with the growth of chain-store operations in the suburban malls, the geographic disparity is less pronounced. There are currently close to 16,000 stores that sell books in the United States. Table IV-1 compares the percentage of total stores in each state to each state's ranking on several key measures: the state's proportion of the adult population of the country, its percentage of adults who have graduated from college, its per capita income as a percentage of the U.S. per capita income. Rank order correlations find extremely high positive relationships between the percentage of bookstores in each state and its college graduate proportion as well as its total adult population, with correlations of .96 and .97, respectively. However, the relationship between number of bookstores and per capita income is rather weak, at .26.[3] Thus, it may be argued that bookstores have followed population concentrations and education levels, with income being a less crucial determinant of location.

THE INDIVIDUAL BOOK BUYER

The determination of true buying motives for any product is a very imprecise exercise. Economic factors are interwoven with sociological and psychological variables. Even studies of buying motives are suspect, since consumers often cannot articulate any conscious reason for purchasing a particular good or brand. Even when the buyer does know why, he or she is not always willing or able to make it known within the design of a study.

Nonetheless, it is useful for the publisher, as well as the

---

[3]Rank-difference correlation coefficient, r'. A perfect congruence between the two measures would be 1.00, whereas a completely inverse relationship would be −1.00. A r' of 0.00 is interpreted as absolutely no relationship.

bookseller, to know why buyers purchase books in general or a specific title. Although research may not yet (or hopefully ever) be able to predict the buying behavior of an individual, it can provide information on aggregate consumer behavior, much as actuarial tables can accurately predict general life expectancies without pinpointing individuals.

Most research has shown a high degree of congruence between educational attainment and book readership (which includes library users as well as book purchasers). Income and occupation also correlate highly with reading and buying of books, but since income and occupation are themselves generally considered to be a product of educational attainment, education must be rated as the more pronounced determinant. A study published in 1946 by Link and Hopf reported that 71% of college-educated respondents were "active" readers, whereas only 10% were nonreaders. On the other hand, only 25% of those who did not go beyond grade school were active readers; whereas 56% were nonreaders. The study also showed a similar, though less pronounced, trend between active reading and higher income. Of the respondents classified as upper income level, 53% were college educated, 37% completed high school, and 10% went only as far as grade school, with the inverse pattern being found for lower-income respondents.[4]

TWO STUDIES

Table IV-2 compares the results of two more recent studies of buyers. One, conducted by now defunct *Book Week* over a six-month period in 1963-1964, consisted of almost 1000 telephone surveys a month in three cities (New York, San Francisco, and Washington, DC). Respondents were asked if they had purchased any books in the past month. Those who had were asked several further questions regarding the type, use, and place of their purchases.[5]

---

[4] H.C. Link and H.A. Hopf, *People and Books* (New York: Book Manufacturers Institute, 1946).

[5] Brown, op. cit.

TABLE IV-2: Two Studies of Book Purchasers[1]

	BOOK WEEK (1963-64) .(bought book in past month)	KIPI (1975) (bought in past six months)
1. Hardback	51%	19%
Paperback	49	81
2. Use:		
Personal	84	90
Gift	16	8
Other	—	2
3. Where bought:	(a specific book)	(stores used in past six months)
Full service bookstore	33%	45%
Paperback store	9	84
Department store	7	20
Newsstand, supermarket, stationery, chain, etc.	31	24
Book club	14	7
Mail order	6	4
College store	Not included	32

4. Income   (of purchasers who bought books)

$10,000 and over	60%	$20,000 and over	32%
$ 7,500-9,999	46	$15,000-19,999	21
$ 5,000-7,499	35	$10,000-14,999	12
under $5,000	24	$ 7,500-9,999	12
		under $7,500	4
		N.R.	19

A somewhat different approach was used in a survey conducted by Knowledge Industry Publications, Inc. (KIPI). Undertaken in April 1975, only actual book purchasers were interviewed, following an observed purchase in five randomly selected bookstores in the Philadelphia metropolitan area. A major difference in the KIPI study was that every book purchaser was questioned, including children. This, of course, is reflected in the education and age demographics and probably inflates the lower education and age levels, since many buyers were students.

Nonetheless, the juxtaposition of the two surveys confirms a number of book-buying trends, while highlighting the change in another. In the *Book Week* survey, purchases were about evenly divided between hardcover and paperback books. This is entirely consistent with an identical breakdown in U.S. Commerce Dept. figures for 1967. In the 1975 study, book buyers estimated that

5. Education   (of those who bought books)

College graduate	63%	46%
Some college	55	20
High school graduate	33	23
Some high school	22	} 11
Less than high school	7	

6. Age   (of those who bought books)

18-24	53%	under 18	8%
25-34	48	18-25	29
35-49	44	26-34	23
50 and over	24	35-54	29
		55 and over	10

7. Sex and race

Male	40		43
Female	39		57
		White	87
		Black and other	13

8. 54% of books bought   46% of books bought
   by top 9% of purchasers   by top 10% of purchasers

[1] For questions 4 through 7, inclusive, percentages for the *Book Week* study indicate the proportion in each category who bought books. That is, in # 1, 60% of those in the $10,000 and over income bracket bought a book. In the KIPI study, percentage is that for the proportion of the entire sample, since *all* those surveyed were book buyers. Thus, for example, 32% of the sample had family incomes of $20,000 or more.

SOURCE: *Publisher's Weekly*, May 11, 1964.
Knowledge Industry Publications, Inc., 1975.

over four-fifths of their book purchases in the previous six months had been paperback. Recent U.S. Commerce Dept. estimates for the total industry indicate a 75%/25% split favoring the paperbacks. The KIPI study found somewhat fewer books given as gifts, although the purchase period included the Christmas season. Ninety percent of the purchases were for personal use, though, of these, 13% were for formal education requirements, and 15% were for business or work.

Consistent with the increase in the proportion of paperback books bought, 84% of the respondents in the KIPI survey claimed to have made book purchases in a paperback book store. Of the respondents, 32% used a college book store, a category that had been omitted in the earlier study.

The KIPI study further showed a statistically significant relationship between years of formal education and claimed book purchases, despite the inclusion of students. Of those who were college graduates or beyond, 47% had purchased 24 or more books in the previous six months, whereas only 16% of those who did not go beyond high school purchased this volume. However, the study could not provide a statistically significant finding for income and book purchasing, to some extent because 19% of the sample would not answer the question on family income. One other intriguing explanation could be that as more books are published in less expensive mass market editions, those with lower incomes are in a better position to buy books in this format. The complete KIPI survey is contained in Appendix A.

In looking over the sources from which these book purchasers bought, relatively few purchasers belonged to book clubs and even fewer bought books through the mail. These were people who did have access to bookstores and relied on them heavily. Naturally the survey was oriented to bookstore patrons since respondents were selected from actual customers.

When requested to name the factors that influenced them to make their purchase at the particular bookstore in which they were interviewed, surprisingly few purchasers mentioned any sort of service-oriented rationale (Table IV-3). Some buyers came because a store was convenient to their home (e.g., in a suburban mall), or place of work (e.g., a downtown location). But the most frequently cited factor (43%) was the selection of books offered. This is consistent with the responses for the next question (Table

---

TABLE IV-3: Factors Influencing Purchase in Particular Bookstores

Which of these factors, or others not listed, were most important in your decision to purchase these books at this particular store?

1.	Services offered by this bookstore (e.g., special orders, credit, knowledge of the stock)	8%
2.	Selection offered	43
3.	Convenience of the store to home	16
4.	Convenience of the store to work	24
5.	Price of the books	3
6.	Other	6
		100%

SOURCE: KIPI Study of book buyers.

IV-4), asking the source of information customers could identify in learning about the specific book or books they had just purchased. Almost half of those asked claimed to have come into the store with no particular selection in mind, but made their purchases as the result of browsing. Recommendations by friends or others also played a significant role in many choices, but recommendations by sales help and advertisements were seldom cited as reasons (although measuring the true effect of the latter would necessitate a more sophisticated research design).

In deciding on their "spontaneous" purchases, however, many subjects elaborated on their decision-making process with comments such as, "I've read books by this author before and like him/her," or, "I just like science fiction books and this looked good." Others claimed to come in regularly to check the remainder tables (in those stores that carried them) for new additions that they might find to their liking.

Thus, a clear pattern emerges from this limited sample. Of those who are already book buyers by the very fact that they had at least purchased a book during the period of the survey, the tendency is to choose a particular title based on the whim of the moment. Many potential customers were observed to come into the stores, walk around for 15 minutes or more, then depart empty-handed — evidently nothing sparked their interest. But others would browse, pick up several books, replace others, and end up purchasing one book or more. Of course, some customers

TABLE IV-4: Sources of Information Used in Purchase Decision

Which of these sources of information did you use in deciding to buy each book you just purchased? (Could mention more than one)

	% of total responses
1. Recommended by sales help	2%
2. Recommended by a friend, relative, associate	21
3. Book review	11
4. Advertisement	4
5. Browsing	47
6. Bought at request of someone	6
7. Other	9
	100%

SOURCE: KIPI Study of book buyers.

came in and asked for a particular title or author, but even many of these people would buy a different or additional book.

Contrasting this study's demographics with national averages, the book buyers exhibit characteristics of greater education and higher income, but of average age. In Pennsylvania, 8.7% of the adult population had completed college as of 1973, compared to 46% in the study. The median income range for the sample of book buyers was $15,000 to $19,999, compared to a median money income for families in the Northeastern states (in 1972) of $11,942. The median age in the Philadelphia SMSA was 28.4 (in 1970), whereas the sample's median was the 26-34 year old range. Book purchasers also split closely between men and women, at 43% and 57% respectively in this survey. On the other hand, blacks and other nonwhites, who make up over 34% of the Philadelphia SMSA population, accounted for only 13% of the book purchasers. Conceivably, however, a survey of book buyers at newsstands, supermarkets, or drugstores might have resulted in a higher proportion of nonwhites.

Even within a population of book buyers, there were great extremes in purchasing — consistent with the *Book Week* findings. This can be seen in the difference between the mean and median figures for claimed purchases over the preceding six months. The mean, at 27.5, is almost twice the median of 14. Without the top 10% of book purchasers in the sample who accounted for 46% of total books claimed to be purchased, the mean would have been 16.5.

CONCLUSIONS

It is clear from the findings of the KIPI study and industry figures that the future of general book sales is tied closely to the paperback book. Although the price of these books has been edging up over the years, the gap in price between them and the hardcover editions remains substantial. But this should surprise no one who pays even cursory attention to the industry. More significant is the method by which consumers choose their books. General book buying and reading appears to be a habit, just as watching television or knitting may be. Books are an alternative for many as an outlet for their leisure time. Given the major role of spontaneity in choosing a book, it would appear that increasing general book purchasing first requires getting people used to going into bookstores or book departments and becoming more interested in reading. Only then will exposure to book reviews, advertising, recommendations, etc. exert an influence on the actual purchase decision.

V

Getting Books to the Reader: Trade Books

CHANNELS OF DISTRIBUTION

The channel of distribution is the term for the flow of a product from the manufacturer to its intended market. Typically it includes a wholesaler and a retailer, although the wholesaler may be omitted and in the case of many mail order or door-to-door sales, the retailer may also be eliminated. For books, all three channels are used, along with several modifications, as illustrated in Diagram V-1. Each channel represents a physical flow of books from manufacturer to ultimate purchaser. Since each publisher rationally seeks to maximize his distribution and sales at a minimum cost, publishers frequently use multiple channels to reach differing markets. For example, Avon Books used independent distributors to reach the mass market with its rack-sized version of *Watership Down*, but its trade paperback version was sold through trade book and institutional channels.

A study for the Association of American Publishers (AAP) in 1974 reported that about 47.3% of the trade publisher's revenue came from direct sales to bookstores, another 38.5% from sales to wholesalers, 7.5% from direct sales to libraries and schools, 2.3% from chain stores and other mass market outlets buying direct, 1.8% from special sales and premiums, and 2.6% from mail orders. Since libraries spend 85% of their trade book acquisition funds through jobbers (see Table VI-4), it can reasonably be surmised that wholesalers play a minor role in the volume of trade books they supply to retail outlets.

DIAGRAM V-1: Channels of Distribution for General Books

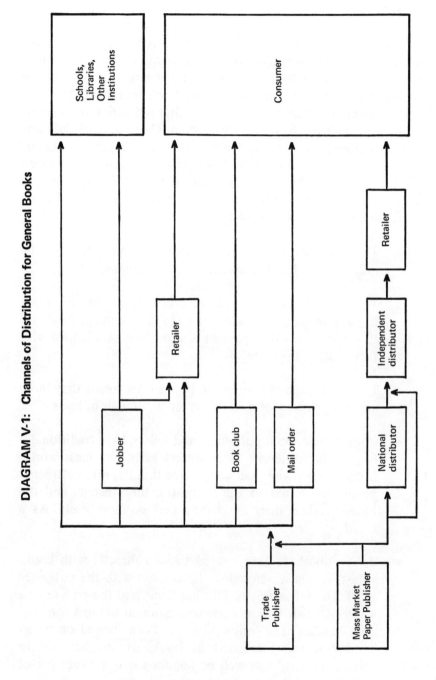

The retailer

The essence of retailing is time and place utility: having the product where and when the consumer wants it. Book publishers have long suffered with the problems of distribution, or as Cheney labeled it in 1931, "the tragedy of the book industry." The root of the trouble is obvious: unlike most other industries, booksellers are blessed with an explosion of product. Currently, 35,000 new titles or editions are appearing each year, increasing the number of titles now in print to beyond 450,000. Conceivably a given individual might want to buy any one of these 450,000 titles at a given moment. The magnitude of the distribution problem is great primarily because of the following reasons:

- The inventory and paperwork needed to keep track of the quantity and location of each title is burdensome;

- To a great extent, individual companies in the book publishing industry have not been large enough to afford the modern computer systems that could have helped with their distribution task;

- The small unit size of most bookstores means that there are many orders for a relatively small number of books;

- Book people, both publishers and sellers, have traditionally been a bit different from others in the business world. Books have always had a mystique that has often attracted people interested in the literature, the prestige, and the image, rather than the hard-nosed business itself. As a result —

- Book publishers have tended to deal directly with booksellers, the latter enjoying the contact with the publisher and his direct salesmen. This has hampered the growth of a wholesale distribution network, common in most consumer industries. The wholesaler has been looked on as an interloper, not interested in books at all, but merely volume. He might as well be handling soap powder for all he cares about books as a precious mission;

- Thus, the industry has never really developed a discount structure that permits a wholesaler to take an attractive margin and still sell to retailers at enough of a discount to allow the retailer to prosper too. This has further perpetuated the system, since the retailer feels that he must deal directly with the publishers to get a discount he can work with;

- Finally, there is the horror of returns, the privilege of a bookseller to return perfectly good, undamaged merchandise that he had ordered and paid for, to the publisher for credit. This is one of the most unique characteristics of the book trade.

Trade book discount structure

The discount is the difference between the manufacturer's suggested list price of a book and what the bookseller, wholesaler, or library pays for it. For the most part, publishers do not have a separate discount structure for jobbers and retailers, basing their discount instead simply on the number of books purchased per order. This, of course, favors the jobber who orders in greater quantity, but multiunit retailers or large retailers can often do almost as well. In most cases, publishers determine discounts for entire categories of books rather than for each title. Adult trade, for example, has a different discount structure than professional books, and mass market paperbacks have a third structure. On the average, the jobber gets about a 5% or 6% greater discount than a retailer, varying slightly from publisher to publisher. A large, national jobber might be able to buy some trade books for as much as 49% to 50% off list.

Volume discount may be construed in two ways. On the one hand, there is the volume of ordering many books of a single title. More frequently, however, trade publishers give their discount based on the total number of books ordered at one time, regardless of the number of titles. A typical schedule of trade book discounts is shown in Table V-1.

A retailer buying from a jobber, however, would face a discount structure with fewer breaks, as shown in Table V-2.

TABLE V-1:   Discount Structure of Trade Publisher to Retail Bookseller

Number of Assorted Titles	Discount
1-4	25%
5-49	40
50-99	41
100-249	42
250-499	43
500-999	44
1000-over	46

A few trade books but most professional books are sold on "short discount." These books, addressed to highly specialized markets, are usually higher priced and are offered to dealers at discounts of 20% to 25%. General retailers often hesitate to carry these books because, even at their higher list prices, their turnover is so slow that they do not justify taking shelf space from potentially higher volume books at regular discounts. Nonetheless, stores whose customers are prone to buy professional books can still do well at the shorter discount. One $25.00 book bought at a 20% discount yields a $5 margin, compared to selling two $6.00 volumes bought at a 40% discount, which results in a $4.80 gross margin.

TABLE V-2:   Trade Book Discount Structure of Jobber to Retail Bookseller

Number of Assorted Titles	Discount
1	net
2-24	20%
25 or more	40%

Discounts are a major factor in analyzing the status of book sales. Compared to most other retail fields, the discount available to retail booksellers is low. This is partially due to the fixed price of books. It has long been the custom of publishers to print the suggested list price on the jacket or cover. This practice saves the bookseller a considerable amount of time, and hence expense, in processing books for the shelf. But it also makes it difficult for a bookseller who offers special services or atmosphere to charge more than a chain store operation.

Although most people understand that they will pay more for a camera in a small photography shop that offers a charge plan, expert advice, special lessons, and the like, than in a cash-and-carry discount operation, that option does not really exist for a book retailer. Other industries, such as much of the clothing business, do not work with a list price system; it is common for the retailer to merely mark up garments 100% over cost. And even in industries that do have suggested list prices, the discount structure typically allows the retailer more leeway for his own pricing structure. In the toy business, for example, larger operations can buy from manufacturers for discounts of 50/5, or an effective 52.5% off, whereas even small units find terms of 40/10 (46%) off list common.

TRADE BOOK DISTRIBUTION

Several book distribution systems have coexisted simultaneously in an uneasy peace. There is the publisher to bookseller channel, and the publisher to jobber to retailer flow; in both cases the retailer then sells to the consumer. However, there is also a direct publisher to consumer link via direct mail. Institutions also buy either directly from the publisher or from a jobber. Thus, competition exists not only within channels, but among them as well.

Although libraries and schools long ago learned to be satisfied in buying from jobbers, booksellers have had almost a pathological affinity for dealing directly with the publishers, a death wish that the publishers gleefully foster. For the fact is, each publisher is interested not in selling *books*, but in selling *his own* books. Of course! A wholesaler, on the other hand, is less committed to a specific publisher; his interest is in volume. If Doubleday has a hot seller or two, the wholesaler would just as soon ship those books out the door than work on stimulating sales for the rather promising book Harper & Row has that so far has failed to catch on, or push a backlist title (an established book that sells year after year such as many dictionaries, cookbooks, or how-to books) that is a steady, but slow seller.

As a result, most of the major publishers have their own sales forces, salesmen (mostly), who ply the territory, pushing their new titles and backlists to retailers, large and small. The smaller publishers will use commissioned representatives, independent personnel who handle several book lines. Either way, the retailer gives an order to each individual publisher and about six weeks later a procession of United Parcel trucks begins delivering a few cartons from each publisher.

In practice, retailers order new titles from publishers, as well as backlist books. They will usually group their orders to justify at least the 40% discount given by publishers for moderate orders. Wholesalers are traditionally utilized when a specific title, a bestseller, is needed quickly.

The role of wholesalers and jobbers

There are approximately 1000 general wholesalers of trade hardcover and paperback books in the United States. Most are small regional firms and many specialize in supplying the library and institutional markets rather than the retailer. A large national jobber, such as Baker & Taylor (division of W.R. Grace & Co.), claims to stock 110,000 to 130,000 titles of the 450,000 titles in print, whereas a medium size jobber such as Ingram will carry 50,000 to 60,000 titles. Nonetheless, this latter figure encompasses over 80% of the titles requested by retailers or libraries.

The wholesaler considers the publisher to be his biggest competitor. "Publishers should publish, wholesalers should distribute," recommends a not-too-disinterested national jobber. Publishers and retailers look askance at wholesalers as just tolerable middlemen but the wholesalers nonetheless provide a major service to both. For the publisher, the wholesaler provides an inventory function, buying his stock and providing a cushion in the pipeline, relieving the publisher of the need to keep bound, unsold books or sheets in a warehouse, tying up cash. A good wholesaler also constitutes a sales force, covering the territory he knows best. Furthermore, by dealing with a relatively small number of wholesalers, the publisher is faced with a smaller amount of paperwork.

There are savings in handling fewer, though individually larger, orders.

By the same token, the retailer can minimize his own processing and handling costs through the use of a jobber. Instead of dealing with 50 or 100 publishers, with invoices to pay to each, shipping cost on small lots, and returns to each, most books can be purchased through one or two wholesalers, minimizing handling and leading to direct savings in labor expense. Diagrams V-2 and V-3 illustrate this role function, vis-a-vis the publisher and retailer. For example, in Diagram V-2 each publisher must deal with four retailers. If this were the total universe of publishers and sellers, there would be 12 contacts (three publishers with each of four sellers). Each new bookseller would add three more contacts. By using a middleman, in Diagram V-3, the number of contacts is cut to seven, one from each publisher to the wholesaler, one from the wholesaler to each bookseller. The addition of each new bookstore would add only one new contact. Thus, the addition of one more bookseller in Diagram V-2 would cause an increase for the industry of three times the number of business contacts as in Diagram V-3.

For the retailer, the key function of the wholesaler is service. Most wholesalers are able to provide an order to a customer within a week of its receipt, as compared to the four to six weeks that a publisher usually takes, especially on orders away from the East Coast.

But quick service has more wide-ranging economic impact for retailers than many of them realize. In being able to supply many titles on short notice, the jobber can, in effect, provide an inventory function for the bookseller as well – a welcome feature in many small businesses with limited capital and space. A savvy bookseller could then place a minimum order with the publisher for an initial stock and wait to see which titles sell well. Later he could use the services of the wholesaler for a speedy resupply of just those titles that are moving successfully, without being burdened by having dollars tied up in volumes on the shelves. It all sounds tidy, yet wholesalers remain an underutilized channel for retailers. This seems to be due to four reasons:

1. The unique book industry return policy. Publishers move

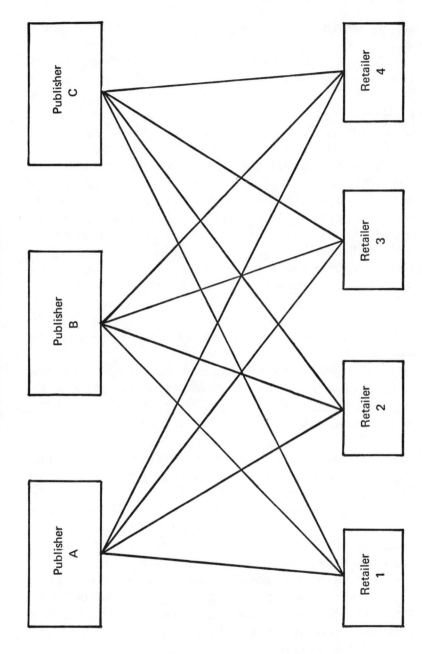

DIAGRAM V-2:   Publishers to Retailers

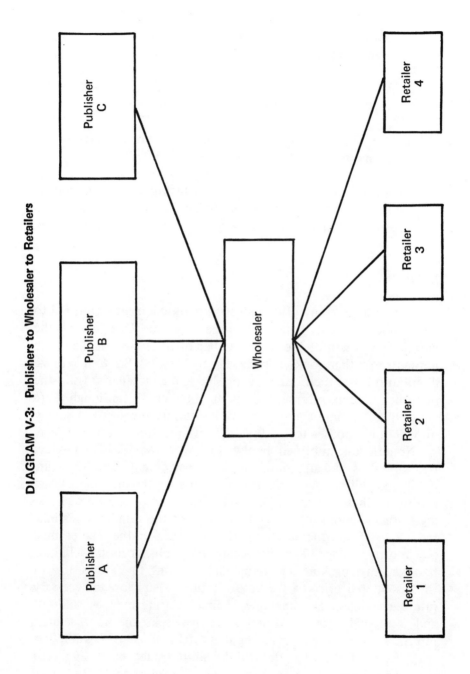

DIAGRAM V-3: Publishers to Wholesaler to Retailers

books into the store by agreeing to take back, for full credit, any unsold copies;

2. The previously mentioned desire of the bookseller for close contact with the publisher;

3. An abandonment by the wholesaler of the retailer for many years;

4. The old-fashioned, unaggressive techniques of the wholesalers, both in marketing themselves to retailers and in handling their own inventory and paperwork requirements.

Returns

Unlike almost any other industry, booksellers are permitted to return books actually bought from the publisher. This policy is the natural outgrowth of the large number of titles published and the limited room that booksellers have in their stores. So, to maximize distribution of their titles and share the retailer's risk, the publisher accepts returned books at 100% credit (although there are frequently time and paperwork limitations involved). A survey of 129 trade houses found that 125 offered this return privilege.

Nonetheless, returned books do cost the bookseller money. His capital is tied up, since, unlike consignment, the books are purchased, billed, and paid for, with the return credited against future purchases from the publisher. The cost of shelving, checking invoices, bookkeeping, and capital cost the retailer an estimated 7% to 15% of the purchase price. In addition, the retailer must pay return postage. This also costs the publisher money: billing, bookkeeping, packing and unpacking amount to 25% to 30% of the discounted price of the book. Returns also cause unnecessary printing expense. For example, a first printing may be sold out and a second printing ordered. Then weeks or months later, returns start coming in, resulting in a total real sale of possibly less than the first printing. Returns to adult trade houses in recent years have been running at about 20%, according to AAP surveys, with trade paperbacks slightly lower. Returns of juvenile books are a modest 6%, reflecting their heavy institutional sale.

The cost to trade publishers alone of handling returns was probably in excess of $15 million in 1974, and may be double that figure. And this is exclusive of transportation cost, cost to the booksellers, and added printing costs. What is more difficult to estimate is the other side of the policy: how many orders were placed and how many books were sold as the result of retailers purchasing titles that they would otherwise have avoided were it not for the return policy?

According to the AAP's figures, trade publishers averaged a return of 17.4% of gross sales in 1976 — very close to the 16.5% level of 1974 (see Table II-5). For 10 major mass market publishers, the average 31.3% return compares to 36.2% in 1973. Returns of 13.6% from 76 book clubs remained close to the figure for the previous year.

Returns are a source of cash for bookstores, allowing them to pay part of their current bills by returning books previously ordered. Some publishers complained that the same mail that brought returns for credit occasionally contained new orders for the very titles that had previously been shipped back!

Publisher/bookseller relations

Trade publishers reach most major bookstore customers through personal sales calls, although small and out-of-the-way stores are reached primarily through catalogues. A major house, such as Doubleday, has nearly 50 store salesmen in addition to a like number visiting schools and libraries. Most larger outlets are visited four times yearly, once in advance of the spring and fall publishing seasons to sell stock and to solicit reorders. Major accounts are visited monthly. Smaller publishers rely on a similar rhythm from commission representatives who may handle books of 10 or 11 publishers simultaneously.

The publisher's representatives prepare for their rounds in sales conferences, at which time editors make presentations of their new titles and give them pep talks. The representatives are armed with dust jackets, sample pages, and summary information on a book's content, information about the author, and perhaps an indication of the potential markets for the title. The good salesman will try to understand his accounts and recommend those titles that fit into that shop's previous sales history.

The fascination of the booksellers with the publisher's representative is recognized in the official *Manual on Bookselling*, published by the American Booksellers Association, the organization of retail bookstores. Richard H. Noyes, currently ABA president and owner of a bookstore, writes that the ideal trade representative "is at least reasonably well educated; a reader, of course . . . He is empathetic with retail bookselling, and knowledgeable about it." The representative, according to Noyes, believes in the basic integrity of the house he represents and serves "as a valuable source of information and scuttlebutt about bookselling and booksellers in his territory, and about interesting developments in the trade in general." The representative usually develops a personal relationship with the bookseller. The representative can thus be a valuable resource for the bookseller in trying to determine which titles, out of the thousands of alternatives available, he should buy. He also provides feedback to the publisher in assessing what is going on "out there," and helping editors to determine the direction of future titles.

Obviously spending an hour or two with each representative is exhilarating to the bookseller and may provide useful information in making purchase decisions. But from the bookseller's point of view this process must be weighed against the alternative of spending more time reading trade reviews and news on his own, and then making up orders dispassionately, not while a friendly salesman is sitting there with pen in hand.

WHOLESALERS IN THE RETAIL MARKET

Wholesaling has always seemed inadequate in the trade field. In 1930, there were only three major wholesalers who together accounted for nearly 25% of publishers' sales. Although the East Coast and the Chicago area were covered by these jobbers, the rest of the country suffered. In the post-war period, even these jobbers lost interest in the retail market, concentrating instead on the library and institutional customers. This market, they believed, was a rapidly growing field and one that promised greater profit. Instead of merely supplying books, the library jobber supplied a service: cataloguing, jacketing, ordering and processing books from a multitude of publishers, and providing a single invoice for this service. And whereas a jobber would have to offer a retailer 35% to 40% off list to be even marginally competitive with the publishers, he can make more money by offering libraries 33 1/3% off trade titles, whereas the publishers charge libraries anywhere from net to 20% off.

As wholesalers saw it, retailers were giving publishers the large, original orders and leaving them to handle the less profitable fill-in orders. So, they concentrated on the library market, further driving the retailer and publisher together. At the same time, those jobbers who did continue to specialize in retail business impressed many retailers as being unreliable. Inventory controls were minimal, so that when a bookseller sent in an order, he had no idea which books he would be shipped and which would be out of stock. Moreover, jobbers have been faulted for failing to provide aggressive sales personnel. What sales efforts they engaged in were more oriented toward opening up new accounts than to selling books. And finally, as regional concerns, jobbers could not do the volume of business necessary to support a large inventory of many backlist titles, so booksellers still had to depend on the publishers for these.

The potential

The common wisdom (and mathematics) holds that the shortest distance between two points is a straight line. Thus, trade publishers and booksellers have worked together, bypassing the despised middleman. The publisher sells to the retailer at a lower discount than he would to a jobber, the retailer still ends up with a higher margin than he would by using a wholesaler. What this common sense and Euclidean analysis ignores, however, is the *cost* of moving the distance between two points. It may well be that the sad state of wholesale operations, the input of the publisher's representatives, the return policy, and the greater margins did make the publisher-retailer channel financially attractive for all. Such would not be the case if wholesalers were more efficient and could provide retailers with superior services.

The key to breakthroughs in wholesaler service is, not surprisingly, technology. But none of it is brand new, only freshly applied to the staid ways of trade book distribution. Three tools are involved: the telephone, the computer, and microfiche.

There is nothing novel in using electronic processing and storage systems to control inventory. Yet this use is innovative in trade book distribution. Although jobbers are increasingly using computers to handle inventory and ordering, Ingram Book Co., headquartered in Nashville, Tennessee, has taken the lead in keeping a running inventory of its inventory of more than 15,000 trade and mass market titles. Ingram's system not only makes its inventory control more efficient but it lets its customers know which books they can expect to receive when they order and which will have to be back ordered — or requested from another wholesaler.

How Ingram works

1. The computer

Each day, the Ingram computer file is updated to reflect new shipments received. Twice daily, at 11:00 AM and 6:00 PM, orders received from customers are batch processed. For each customer's order, a picking list is generated, with titles printed out in the order that conforms to the arrangement of the books on the shelves in Ingram's warehouses. At the same time, mailing labels are produced, and total inventory levels for each title are adjusted to reflect that order. Most orders received by 10:30 AM are thus processed and shipped by common carrier the same day. If any items from a customer's previous order were out of stock (and if the customer indicated he still would want the books when available), the computer automatically adds these titles to the picking list. Later, the computer generates an invoice based on the actual shipment.

2. The microfiche

The computer is also instrumental in the functioning of another key facet of the Ingram system: microfiche listings of current inventory for subscribing retailers. The role of the fiche is to enable retailers to have current information on Ingram stock, as well as other relevant data. Although the same information could be provided merely by hardcopy reproduction of the computer printout, the fiche form permits more rapid delivery of and access to the data. Three four-by-six inch microfiche cards are generated each Saturday, showing data that are therefore current as of Monday morning, when the fiche arrive by mail to each subscriber. Holding the equivalent of over 450 pages of information, the fiche contain:

— Ingram's entire hardcover and paperback inventories, including quantity on hand and quantity on order, available by publisher, author, and title indexes;

— Trade information, such as upcoming author appearances on network and syndicated television shows, upcoming reviews in national magazines, movie and television tie-ins. All this helps the bookseller in anticipating future customer demands and aids him in making ordering decisions;

— Bestseller lists — an early line on titles on the *New York Times* list, as well as Ingram's top movers based on actual sales figures;

— A special breakout of new titles that the jobber received the previous week, as well as a special list of new books that Ingram itself believes are going to be good sellers;

— Status of important books, showing which are back in stock or now out of stock, books on which the publication date has been delayed, postponed, or on which the price has been changed.

This information is valuable in aiding retailers in numerous ways. It gives them significantly better information than they ever had as the basis for making decisions. They know they can get what they order with a high degree of certainty, and whether items they ordered previously are now in stock. They can predict demand for top sellers better and can advise their customers accordingly when asked "When will X be out?" They can take special orders for customers knowing if their supplier has the book — or if not, avoid a promise of early delivery when it can't be so ordered. The cost of Ingram's service is currently $125 annually, including a microfiche reader and full service.

3. The telephone

Nothing is startling about the use of the telephone except for the addition of a WATS number, to encourage customers to call, 24 hours a day. Callers using toll-free WATS, however, must give their orders by the Ingram title code. This cuts order costs considerably, not to mention the retailer's phone bill. The order made over WATS must also be for a minimum of 50 books.

The combination of fiche and telephone also saves Ingram money since the jobber does not get an order from a customer unless the book is in stock, cutting processing time further. Ingram is refining the system by adding video display terminals. This will allow order takers to get immediate customer identification, and credit and billing information, as well as to check inventory status of any book.

As a result of these economies, Ingram is able to compete more effectively with publisher-offered discounts. Besides the basic 40% discount, customers whose total order is 300 books or more get an additional 1.2% off on any orders of five copies of the same title.

The impact of the Ingram system can be evaluated from the viewpoint of the publishers, retailers, and Ingram itself. In its few years of operation (it started in 1973), the microfiche system has acquired over 1500 customers, including 30 to 40 publishers, far exceeding Ingram's initial expectations and making the fiche system profitable on its own. It has enabled Ingram to grow from a small, regional wholesaler with $5 million in sales in 1969 to one of the top jobbers in the country, with an estimated $75-$80 million in sales in 1977. Ingram's inventory turnover of six times annually also exceeds the industry average.

For retailers, the fiche, telephone, quick delivery system has provided the potential to increase turnover by as much as 100%, from the 2x-3x average to 4x. It appears to have increased the hardcover business of customers, to the point where one Southern proprietor, formerly dealing only in paperbacks, could claim that 45% of his sales were now in hardback, despite devoting only 10% of his unit stock to these titles. At the same time, there are reports of dramatic improvements in returns (which Ingram accepts). To Ingram, returns are about 8%, but its own returns to publishers run only 2%, including mass market paperbacks.

Sessler's, the major Philadelphia full-service bookstore, claims that subscribing to the Ingram package is radically changing its purchasing philosophy. Before buying from Ingram, Sessler's purchased 90% of its books from the publishers, filling in only occasionally from a New York jobber, Dimondstein. By having access to the microfiche information and the WATS number, Sessler's has increased jobber orders to 25% of its volume. It gets delivery within three days and knows in advance what will be in the boxes. "We would use anyone who could provide us with the books we need," claims Sessler's chief book buyer. But it replaced its former jobber with Ingram because the latter has far better control over what's in stock.

Publishers subscribe to the Ingram fiche service so that they can better monitor the movement of their titles. Harper & Row, for example, finds the information helpful and is encouraged about its use in broadening the market for books.

Once a system such as Ingram's is operational, additional services for the retailer become possible. One possibility is an automatic reorder program for retailers, whereby the jobber could keep an actual inventory record for each participating customer. Booksellers, using point-of-sale recording devices (sophisticated cash registers), could then send their tapes, containing a record of all sales by inventory number, to the jobber each week. The jobber would return a printout to the retailer containing information on which books are low or out of stock. Depending on the customer's wishes, the jobber could automatically ship a quantity of these titles or await a specific order from the retailer. Such a system would give the small retailer the benefits of an expensive computerized inventory control system while providing the jobber with a fuller role in the distribution network. Publishers would derive maximum benefits, however, only if more of the major wholesalers provided a similar service. Under those conditions, a publisher who was trying to decide, for example, on an additional printing of a title could tell at a glance what the inventory level was in the wholesale pipeline. Overstocked wholesalers in areas where the book was selling slowly might be asked to return some, so that they might be resold to others who are having greater success. And print orders could be more finely tuned.

A system such as Ingram's naturally lends itself to great economies of scale as well as the potential for flexibility. With a full-time programming staff of five and computer costs of $5000 to $6000 a month, Ingram can double its current volume without adding to its EDP facility. Such an expansion already took place, with the addition in 1975 of a satellite warehouse in Jessup, Maryland. Although all orders are still placed through Nashville, picking lists for customers in New England, the Middle Atlantic States, plus Maryland, Delaware, Virginia, West Virginia, and the District of Columbia are transmitted, via telephone lines, to a printer at the Jessup facility. Thus, orders for these customers are sent by common carrier a shorter distance, providing two to three day service in most cases. Ingram plans to add further warehouses, with the goal of having one within 300 miles of any customer, yet with all the processing and billing remaining in Nashville. And, as the industry moves toward the use of International Standard Book Numbers (ISBN) for ordering (see Chapter XIII), the computer can continue to accept Ingram's own order numbers from customers (to maintain its competitive uniqueness) while converting them to ISBN in generating reorders to the publishers. By purchasing Raymar in 1976, the major West Coast jobber, Ingram is truly national.

Significance

This description of Ingram's innovative system may sound more like a promotional piece from its sales department than an objective analysis. The fact is that Ingram has made a number of major improvements in the distribution of trade books (and mass market books) to the retail bookseller and deserves any kudos — and profits — that may come its way. Ingram has not solved all the problems; although perhaps 80% of the volumes sold can be covered in an inventory of 15,000 titles, there is still the need for processing special orders for the other 20% of the titles that retailers need. This burden still falls on the publishers and booksellers, although Ingram has an additional 45,000 titles for its library clientele that can eventually be hooked into its retail system. Sessler's, the Philadelphia retailer, finds it must still send out 50 to 60 letters a week with special orders to publishers for many of the classic and backlist titles that its customers request. Such titles do not generate a large enough volume for Ingram or most other jobbers to stock.

Nonetheless, Ingram has blazed the trail, showing what can be accomplished without relying on radical remedies or organizing the entire industry in a distribution cooperative. Its system combines common business practices and available technology with the willingness to make the necessary investment. Yet Ingram still has to convince retail booksellers that they can actually increase their profits by using the information available through the fiche system and raising inventory turnover even though there is a 1% or 2% difference in discount between Ingram and what the publisher offers directly.

ISBN

An industry-wide attempt to improve the accuracy and speed of handling orders, inquiries, billing and identification is the International Standard Book Number (ISBN). This is a unique number assigned to each book and edition. At a time when there is a rapid proliferation of titles, often with similar names, the ISBN provides a way of identifying each individual book.

For wholesalers, ISBNs afford a precise method of ordering, as well as a far more exact means of identifying titles for checking as they are received at distribution warehouses. Furthermore, if publishers could be persuaded to put ISBNs on the spines of book jackets, the accuracy of wholesalers' order picking, inventory, and general stock management could be measurably improved. Currently, the numbers are usually printed on the copyright page, but some publishers also put them on the lower righthand corner of the back of the dust jacket or paperback cover.

For publishers, the outside location of the ISBN can likewise help in identification for checking in returns.

Major library systems are using or implementing ISBNs in their data bases, whether or not they are computerized. For large university systems, in which book requests are initiated by many sources, the ISBN is a way to be sure that orders for the same titles are not inadvertently duplicated. And as the electronic transmission of data from one computer to another becomes more of an economic reality, a common data base entered by ISBNs will become an absolute necessity.

Despite these advantages, the ISBN system has been slow to

catch on. Major wholesalers such as Baker & Taylor say only a small fraction of incoming orders contain the ISBN. In the institutional market this reflects the inertia of many thousands of libraries who must be persuaded to convert to ISBNs for ordering. For retail-oriented jobbers such as Ingram, bookstore ordering by ISBN would impair the uniqueness of a computerized system based on Ingram's own ordering numbers.

ECONOMICS OF TRADE BOOK DISTRIBUTION
FOR THE PUBLISHER

Much of this chapter has concentrated on the economics of trade book distribution from the standpoint of wholesalers and booksellers. And indeed from their perspective, improving the jobber-retailer links holds out promise of better inventory management, increased sales and higher profits.

But what about from the publisher's viewpoint? Larger publishers obviously believe the way to maximize profits is to push their books aggressively by direct selling, thereby guaranteeing that their cookbook, analysis of the Bermuda Triangle, guide to transcendental meditation or spy novel is bought by the bookstore, rather than some other publisher's. And, in fact, the profitability of trade publishers (or any publishers) is strongly correlated with the publisher's ability to control its own distribution, whether through salesmen, mail order selling or whatever, as well as to spread his fixed editorial and overhead costs over a wider range of titles.

Although profit margins are frequently correlated with size, this is not always the case. In 1976, for example, the six trade publishers with sales of over $15 million had a pretax profit of 4.5%, well above the margin of very small (under $1 million sales) publishers, which had a .9% margin, and medium size publishers ($5 to $15 million), which had a .8% profit. But publishers in the $1 to $5 million range averaged a 4.8% margin in 1976, indicating that modest size need not preclude relatively substantial returns. In general, however, smaller publishers tend to spend a greater percentage of their revenue for editorial, production, and marketing expenses than the larger establishments.

It would appear that increasing sales through wholesalers is an obvious way for the smaller publisher to cut his costs, as well as to reduce some of the high overhead and order processing expenses associated with dealing directly with a large number of retailers. Nevertheless, small trade publishers are nervous about such a strategy, feeling — rightly so, in a number of instances — that the wholesalers are not interested in doing business with them.

Actually, large publishers have something to gain from dealing with wholesalers too. Not only would cutting down on the volume of orders from bookstores cut publishers' fulfillment costs, but better inventory management and ordering procedures by the stores would improve retailers' profits and increase the total volume of industry sales. Since larger publishers have the resources to bid for and publish more popular books, they would be better placed to take advantage of a general industry movement toward higher unit sales of fewer titles.

The counter-argument to this analysis is that many worthwhile books will not be published if booksellers pay even more attention to fast-moving titles. Yet the fact is that stores are already feeling their way in this direction, and the constant cry at ABA meetings and other publisher-bookseller get-togethers is "give us fewer titles" and "why must 12 different publishers come out with books on house plants or yoga?"

The very nature of trade publishing, with its emphasis on editorial verve, creativity and lack of formulas, militates against a takeover of this branch of the book business by a few giant publishers. Only two trade publishers come close to having as much as 10% each of the total market. And the five leading firms have an estimated 37% of the market — a far smaller degree of concentration than exists in mass market paperbacks, college or reference book publishing.

Table V-3 shows estimated sales of the five largest trade publishers.

It should be pointed out, nonetheless, that the recession of 1974-75 proved to be a painful time for smaller trade publishers who were under-captalized — thus encouraging mergers with larger houses that had more solid finances. In 1975 E.P. Dutton was acquired by the Dutch firm, Elsevier Publishing, and Viking Press sold a controlling interest to Pearson Longman Ltd., the British publishing and printing conglomerate.

TABLE V-3:   Sales of the Five Largest Trade Publishers, 1976

Publisher	Sales (in millions)	% Share of Trade Market
1. Random House	$55.0	10%
2. Doubleday	50.0	9.1
3. Harper & Row	42.0	7.6
4. Simon & Schuster	35.0	6.4
5. Wm. Morrow	20.0	3.6

SUMMARY

Several distribution channels coexist for trade books, the most important being publishers selling to bookstores which sell to book buyers. A stronger wholesaler network might benefit both retailers and publishers, through speedier order processing and improved inventory turnover, but this has been resisted by bookstores unwilling to give up gross margin, and by publishers anxious to retain the direct selling approach. Ingram Book Co.'s innovative inventory information system illustrates the advantages accruing to bookstores from a more systematic buying procedure.

Traditional discount and returns policies have similarly hampered the development of more efficient distribution techniques. Gross margins in bookselling are low by other retail standards, and discourage price discounting and aggressive merchandising. The 100% returns policy prevents otherwise desirable inventory clearance sales and encourages bookstores to order books that they should avoid in the first place.

Though more attention to the fundamentals of distribution might reduce the glut of new titles issued annually, smaller publishers will not disappear if the industry becomes more efficient. The nature of trade publishing makes it unlikely the business will ever be heavily concentrated in just a few publishers' hands.

VI

Getting Books to the Reader: Libraries

LIBRARY BOOK BUDGETS

Libraries — public, university, school, and special — represent an enormous market for the nontextbook publishers. Recent estimates place total library acquisitions at almost $260 million in 1976. A survey undertaken by a combined AAP/ALA (American Library Association) task force in late 1974 found that 25% of the 61 publishers responding attributed 70% or more of their total sales to the library market.

There are more libraries than bookstores in the United States and in many ways the two are competitors for the attention of the reading public. There are over 8700 public libraries, of which 11% have annual book acquisition budgets in excess of $25,000. But of the 1667 four-year college and university libraries, 58% have book budgets greater than $25,000. In addition, there are more than 1000 two-year college libraries, more than 7700 special libraries (technical, law, business, government, etc.). In 1976, the library market for domestically published books represented about 8% of total publisher revenues from books in the United States.

Table VI-1 further shows that libraries purchased an estimated 22% of all trade books. It is quite likely that libraries absorb even a higher percentage of those books published in small quantities and in fact are the major reason why many of them can be published at all. About 32% of university press books and almost one-fifth of the professional books end up on library shelves.

Not counted in the usual census of libraries are the 67,000 school libraries, most of which came into being with the infusion of federal funds in the 1960s. As charted in Table VI-2, school libraries spend more than any other type of library and purchased over half the total unit volume of books (since almost a third of their purchases are concentrated in relatively low priced juvenile titles). However, since federal funds for the schools have reached a plateau, projections to the end of the 1970s indicate that the greatest growth in expenditures will be in the public libraries, which can expect substantial increases in dollar purchases and even a modest growth in number of volumes purchased. For the library market as a whole, nonetheless, expenditures will not likely keep pace with the rising cost of books, resulting in an actual decrease in the number of units purchased.

TABLE VI-1:   Domestic Library Acquisitions as Percentage of Total U.S. Book Sales, 1976

	Percent of Total
All Trade	22%
Juvenile	24
Professional	18
Mass market paperback	1
University press	32

SOURCE: Book Industry Study Group, *Book Industry Trends, 1977;* Association of American Publishers, Industry Statistics, 1976

Moreover, books face stiff competition for the library dollar from other publications. One of the most interesting facts to come out of the Book Industry Study group was the high percentage of the library budget going for journals (in the case of academic and special libraries) and audiovisual materials (in the case of school libraries). Books' share of total library acquisitions was estimated to be 45% in 1972-73, and only in public libraries did book purchases account for more than 50% of library buying. When library budgets get squeezed, it is often the book budget that gets cut first, since libraries feel they must give priority to serials in order to maintain the continuity of their collections.

Through the end of 1981, it is estimated that price inflation will account for the entire 63% increase in dollar sales of trade

TABLE VI-2: Estimated Acquisition by U.S. Libraries of Domestically Published Books, Selected Years, 1974-1981 (millions of $ and units) Fiscal Year Ending June 30

Type of Library	1974		1976		1978*		1981*		% change 1974-1981	
	$	Units	$	Units	$	Units	$	Units	$	Units
College and University	$115.6	14.40	$122.9	12.25	$130.7	11.12	$166.7	11.66	44.2%	(19.0%)
% of total	24.0	11.5	24.8	11.8	25.9	12.4	26.6	12.9		
Public	131.3	30.37	148.2	28.29	156.4	26.53	196.4	27.90	49.6	(8.1)
% of total	27.2	24.2	30.0	27.3	30.9	29.6	31.4	30.8		
Special	51.2	4.97	59.6	4.67	69.0	4.64	89.9	4.98	75.6	0.2
% of total	10.6	4.0	12.0	4.5	13.7	5.2	14.4	5.5		
School	184.4	75.61	164.0	58.36	149.2	47.43	173.4	46.10	(7.5)	39.0
% of total	38.2	60.3	33.2	56.3	29.6	52.9	27.7	50.9		
Total	482.5	125.35	494.7	103.57	505.3	89.72	626.4	90.64	29.0	(27.7)
% of total	100.0	100.0	100.0	99.9	100.1	100.0	100.1	100.0		

* Projection

NOTE: 1. Percentage totals may not equal 100.0% due to rounding.
2. Expenditures at library cost of materials, exclusive of any cataloging costs.

SOURCE: Book Industry Study Group, Report No. 3, Nov. 1976. (This report has been subsequently updated by "Library Acquisitions — A Look into the Future," 1977.)

TABLE VI-3: Estimated Acquisitions by U.S. Libraries by Category of Domestically Published Books, 1973-1976 (millions of $ and units)

	1973 $	1973 units	1974 $	1974 units	1975 $	1975 units	1976 $	1976 units	% change 1973-1976 $	% change 1973-1976 units
All Trade	$103.2	41.0	$114.8	44.5	$129.3	41.4	$128.5	40.0	24.5%	(2.4%)
% of total	36.4	51.6	41.5	56.8	41.3	55.1	38.9	53.1		
Juvenile	21.8	11.3	22.6	11.9	31.6	13.0	30.1	11.3	38.1	0.0
% of total	7.7	14.2	8.2	15.2	10.0	17.3	9.1	1.5		
Professional	106.9	19.3	85.0	14.9	88.0	14.1	101.1	15.8	(5.4)	(18.1)
% of total	37.7	24.3	30.8	19.0	28.1	18.8	30.6	21.0		
Mass market paperback	3.8	6.1	4.0	5.9	4.6	5.8	5.6	5.9	55.3	(3.3)
% of total	1.3	7.7	1.4	7.5	1.5	7.7	1.7	7.8		
University press	15.3	2.9	15.4	2.8	15.7	2.2	17.3	2.4	13.1	(17.2)
% of total	5.4	3.6	5.6	3.6	5.0	2.9	5.2	3.2		
Subscription reference	11.2	0.1	10.8	0.1	11.6	0.0	12.2	0.0	8.9	(100.0)
% of total	4.0	.1	3.9	0.1	3.7	0.0	3.7	0.0		
Other[1]	43.1	10.2	46.3	10.1	64.0	11.7	66.0	11.2	53.1	9.8
% of total	15.2	12.8	16.8	12.9	20.4	15.6	20.0	14.9		
Total	283.5	79.5	276.3	78.3	313.2	75.2	330.7	75.3	10.8	(5.3)
% of total	100.0	100.1	100.0	99.9	100.0	100.1	100.1	100.0		

[1] Includes other AAP categories, as well as small quantities of mass market and subscription reference books.

SOURCE: Book Industry Study Group, *Book Industry Trends, 1977*, Table 1.

books to libraries, with units remaining at the 1973 level. As calculated in Table VI-3, trade books, including juvenile, accounted for almost 39% of all library expenditures in 1976, up slightly from the 1973 level. However, their share of total volumes bought by libraries rose slightly. This is because prices of professional books continued their rapid increase, resulting in the greatest decrease in volumes sold to the libraries. It must be emphasized that all of these are only estimates, but they are being refined annually for the Book Industry Study group, a non-profit firm funded mainly by publishers.

The outlook, therefore, for publishers to the library market suggests a decrease in copies sold from the 1973 level but an increase in dollar sales between 1973 and 1981.

LIBRARY CHANNELS OF DISTRIBUTION

Librarians have two basic options for purchasing books: they can order directly from the publisher or through a jobber. In a few cases, they can buy mass market books from a local independent distributor. Libraries face an even larger problem in buying books than retailers. For the most part, they need only one or two copies of any title, but must generally buy a much greater variety of books than do most booksellers. Even academic libraries serve a heterogeneous audience, readers who need reference works, academic and scholarly books, text materials, as well as a wide variety of adult and juvenile trade titles. Besides scanning newly issued titles, librarians are frequently faced with the need to acquire or replace backlist titles and scholarly reprints. In addition, each book must be processed: catalogued, marked for the shelf, and fitted with a checkout card.

Thus, it should not be surprising, as seen in Table VI-4, that almost 54% of library acquisitions in 1973-74 were made through library jobbers, specialists in meeting the needs of libraries — and at an attractive price. Even this total percentage understates the true reliance on the jobbers for certain categories of books and by certain types of libraries. The myriad of trade and mass market books that a library must cope with is the particular bailiwick of the jobbers, whereas professional books are more likely to come from the publisher. Subscription reference volumes, such as encyclopedias and their updates, come exclusively from the relatively few publishers of these series. Public libraries rely most heavily on the services of the jobber; the special law, business, medical and scientific research libraries are understandably the least dependent.

TABLE VI-4: Channels of Acquisitions by U.S. Libraries for Domestically
Published Books, 1973-74

Category	Publishers & Independent Distributors % Share	Library Jobbers % Share
Trade		
incl. Juvenile	24.6	75.4
Professional	81.5	18.5
Mass Market Paperback	61.5	38.5
University Press	47.2	52.8
Subscription Reference	100.0	—
Other	52.7	47.3
Total	46.6	53.4
Type of Library		
College and University	55.5	44.5
Public	34.5	65.5
Special	72.6	27.4
School	43.2	56.8

NOTE: At library cost of acquisition.

SOURCE: Book Industry Study Group, Report No. 3, "Library
Acquisitions," Table 5.

Direct from publishers

Publishers are quite active in trying to reach the decision-makers in the libraries, although generally with the objective of obtaining the order through the jobbers. Besides sending out seasonal catalogues and special mailing pieces, publishers attend library conventions and meetings where they exhibit their books. Some large publishers have sizable direct marketing sales forces: Doubleday has 45 sales personnel for the school and library market. Yet despite the importance of this area, nearly half of the publishers in the AAP/ALA survey spent less than 20% of their marketing budgets in the pursuit of library business.

The truth is that publishers do not want to be bothered with handling the thousands of small orders the libraries require. Most of the books they do sell directly to the libraries are through blanket-order plans, in which more than half the libraries participate to some degree. Under this arrangement, publishers send the library all new publications or, sometimes, only those in certain fields selected by the library. Most major publishers are involved in the Library of Congress Cataloging in Publication (CIP) program, which helps save librarians time and money in cataloguing books. But they do not pretend to provide the full range of cataloguing and processing services offered by jobbers.

Some publishers sell their books at net price to libraries, which, after all, are technically the final consumer. Most, however, offer short discounts of 10% to 20% off list. It should not be surprising that only 28% of the publishers in the AAP/ALA survey believed that direct sales visits are effective in getting orders; librarians regarded this to be among the least effective sales methods.

The publisher's major role in reaching the library market is in gaining the attention of the purchasers for his list. The vast majority of the publishers issue annual or semiannual catalogues of all their books, as well as separate subject catalogues and frequent flyers. However, surveyed librarians also rated these of average effectiveness. Reviews of books have been deemed the most valuable buying aid for libraries. The AAP/ALA study found that the "very important" factors influencing buying decisions were: favorable reviews, faculty recommendations, and the author's reputation. Deemed "important" were: a title that would fill a gap in the library's collection, an important new work in the field, the appearance of a title on a recommended list or the high literary quality of the book, and the publisher's reputation. Judged "unimportant" were sales visits, exhibits, and bargain prices.

Library jobbers

It is obvious from Table VI-4 that librarians have taken to middlemen with far greater enthusiasm than have retail book-sellers. But the feeling has been mutual: jobbers have found the library market quite profitable. Baker & Taylor, the largest jobber, moved into the library market to the virtually complete abandon-ment of the retail sector, and traditional jobbers to the retailer have broadened their activities in recent years to focus more on the libraries. Admits one top executive at Baker & Taylor, "We felt it was just more profitable than regular wholesaling." (In fall 1975, B&T launched a serious program to once again become a full-line retail jobber.)

Supplying libraries is a very different business from serving retailers. As one example, more than just supplying a product, the library jobber is in the service business: it is the jobber who must order and process books from numerous publishers. Wholesalers who wouldn't think of back ordering a title for a retailer do it as a matter of routine for libraries. They provide cataloguing services at a price that most libraries could not touch, even with new Library of Congress aids and other programs. Jobbers may provide out-of-print searches for hard to find titles.

Moreover, the library jobber is set up to handle the small order. The average number of copies per title in the typical order to Baker & Taylor comes to just over one. But with 40,000 customers, B&T (and others on a lesser scale) is still in the position to place large orders to publishers for many titles, earning volume discounts. Even though few copies per title are requested, the total order from an individual library may be sizable.

The physical arrangement of books in a library jobber's warehouse is quite different from that of a retail jobber. In the latter case, books are arranged by the rate at which they sell, with fast movers being grouped close together to minimize the assem-bling time of each order. The library jobber's stock is arranged by publisher, then author and title. "The process is far more manual," explains an Ingram official. Extensive inventory plus backordering are essential, since libraries want jobbers to fill a total purchase order, rather than sending just those books that are available. Ingram, which claims it can fill 80% of a bookstore's needs from the 15,000 trade titles on its fiche cards, has an additional 45,000 titles in a separate library warehouse, arranged by publisher, for this other market.

Except for new fiction and some bestsellers, libraries do not present jobbers with the same time pressures for acquisitions as do retailers. Thus, the "Micro-Bulletin" service of Ingram, for example, providing libraries with fiche of its library inventory, does not contain the same quantity and on-order information as the retail store fiche. Nonetheless, libraries can get orders filled in one to two weeks.

About 60% of wholesalers offer approval plans, whereby new books are sent automatically to subscribing libraries, with over half of the AAP/ALA surveyed libraries subscribing to such an arrangement. Under these setups, the jobber will profile an individual library's needs. Then, as new books arrive at the jobber's, they will be classified by subject and sent to those libraries whose profiles match up. In the case of Baker & Taylor, such pairing is highly automated.

The irony of the library distribution system is that by going through jobbers, libraries often qualify for a 20%-30% discount on trade titles, rather than the shorter discount offered by publishers. Thus, in making work easier for themselves, libraries generally do better than going directly to the publisher, unlike the retailer who may do slightly better with the publisher on discount alone. The library jobbers are truly a case where everyone makes out better: publishers aren't bothered with piles of small orders, libraries keep their paperwork to a minimum, and wholesalers have a greater spread between their buying and selling price than in the retail market. The increasing competition for library business, combined with the high costs of processing orders, has made this a treacherous field for jobbers in recent years, however. At least two library jobbers have gone out of business: Campbell & Hall, whose assets were bought by Booksmith Distributing Co., and Richard Abel, whose assets were acquired by Blackwell's.

Library jobbers have been moving more eagerly into the mass market paperback business as an expansion of their service — and the recognition that these books are finding an established place in libraries as well as schools. Although wholesalers must be highly selective in what they decide to carry, they are finding a growing interest in such services as prebinding paperbacks into hard covers. Librarians overwhelmingly prefer hardcover titles over paperback when they have the choice, but a number of libraries have discovered the utilitarian approach of buying one or two copies of a title for the permanent collection and, where possible, ordering multiple copies of the paper edition for reserve room or short-term heavy use. Paperbacks, however, may earn short discounts of 10%-20% in quantities (per title) of under 25, with 30% off beyond this level.

Despite their efficiencies, library jobbers have been often faulted for being merely order-takers and processors, rather than aggressive marketers. In private, many wholesalers will agree that they have been too complacent. But since library funding is barely keeping pace with inflation, and with the addition of more competitors into the field, jobbers are beginning to supplement publishers' promotion with their own programs. Ingram offers the aforementioned "Micro-Bulletin." Baker & Taylor began publishing several reviewing magazines for libraries in early 1975, as an added selling tool, though later it eliminated any editorial content and converted the publications to catalogues.

Library Cooperatives

Cooperation among libraries has a long history, but this trend has been accelerating as a result of both rising costs and tight funding. Libraries are thus moved to consolidate where possible to eliminate duplication. This is especially significant when studies show that in some large libraries 80% of the circulation is accounted for by only 3% of the holdings. In establishing inter-library loan networks, libraries hope to share purchases of specialized books, professional titles, and very expensive items, rather than having each individual library buy every title. There have also been proposals to reproduce certain titles, especially journal articles, by photocpying, which publishers regard as constituting copyright infringement. Publishers who are involved in producing these types of books will have to address themselves increasingly to the implications of cooperative purchasing, which may further restrict their market.

CONCLUSIONS

Not many library watchers expect funding for library book acquisitions to decrease in absolute dollar amounts, but the evidence strongly indicates that expenditures will do well to keep level with rising costs. The projection is for trade publishers to suffer least in terms of a decline in number of units sold. On the other hand, professional book publishers face less elasticity of demand for their books, which means they are able to raise prices faster. Thus they can generate substantially more in sales even on reduced volume. Professional and technical book publishers, however, must compete for sales with professional journals, which often have priority in academic or special libraries anxious to maintain complete collections in a given field.

All publishers are competing to sell an ever growing assemblage of titles to the library market, meaning that the average title will be selling fewer copies. Works of commendable quality that depended on the library market to make their publication feasible may not now be published.

As a distribution network, the library jobbers are performing a service that has obvious economic value to both publisher and library. The role of the middleman has been shown to be highly efficient in dealing with small numbers of copies in consolidated shipments to thousands of customers. With almost three-quarters of the libraries' needs being fulfilled by the jobber, the groundwork would seem to exist for expanding the wholesaling function to the retail bookseller.

VII

Getting Books to the Reader:
Mass Market Paperbacks

IMPORTANCE OF PAPERBACK SALES

In 1976, publisher sales of mass market paperback books represented about 9.9% of the total dollar volume of book receipts for the year. This is up from the 5.7% of the industry's sales this format accounted for in 1958, but represents a resumption of increases of market share that slipped slightly in 1974.

The mass market designation stems from the widespread distribution of this form of book to somewhere between 60,000 and 80,000 bookstore, newsstand, chain store, drug, gift, and stationery store outlets. For the most part, the books are a standard 4¼ by 7 inch size and fit into pockets, either wire racks or shelves, built to accommodate them. Compared to other forms of mass media, individual paperback books still do not reach significant numbers of readers. In 1976 only 74 of the approximately 4000 paperback releases were even *printed* in quantities of 1 million copies or more. The big leaders were *Elvis: What Happened* (5 million printed), and *Star Wars* (4 million), both from Ballantine.

The mass market paperback is a new phenomenon relative only to the history of book publishing. Nonetheless, it does date back over 40 years now, having gotten its real start with the highly regarded line of Penguin Books first published in England in 1935 and exported to the United States. The first American paperbacks of this nature were by Pocket Books, established in 1939, followed by Avon in 1941, Popular Library in 1942, and Bantam, founded three years later.

From the start, the mass market paperback publishers were in the business of reprinting books that had been previously published in the traditional hardcover format. The paperback publishers would acquire the rights to reprint by offering the hardcover publisher and author an advance against earned royalties, in exchange for the right to reprint for a fixed term, usually three years.

The paperback publishing industry was able to establish itself over the next three decades as a result of at least three factors. The first was this availability of editorial product, which could be licensed fairly inexpensively (usually an advance was no more than $2000). Perhaps more crucial at this time was the introduction of a new printing process, involving a rubber plate rotary press, which made possible fast, economic production runs. This allowed the paperback books to be printed on much the same economic base as magazines. The third element was the existence of a distribution network of wholesalers of magazines who were willing to distribute the paperback books to their newspaper and magazine accounts. Thus, by tapping this network, the publishers were able to have access to 80,000 outlets to sell their products.

Today, there are a dozen paperback houses of national scope a small number in relation to the total number of book publishers. These paperback houses released 4000 new titles in 1976. The largest by far is Bantam, with the others bunched way behind. Table VII-1 gives estimated market share for 1976.

Although the method of printing has not changed over the years, the overall cost of paper and printing has escalated rapidly. But of more concern to most publishers is the skyrocketing costs for getting the reprint rights to many of the big hardcover titles. Competitive bidding has driven guarantees to over $2 million on occasion and publishers frequently agree to pay sums of over $1 million as a guarantee for reprint rights to best sellers. Even the seemingly mundane *Total Fitness in 30 Minutes a Week* drew a winning bid of $810,700 from Pocket Books. As a result, more paperback houses are putting more original titles onto their lists. Avon, for one, expects to have half its list as original books. Meanwhile, the simplicity of distribution through jobbers has moved to a system of overlapping and more complex relationships between publishers and the retail outlets.

TABLE VII-1:   Largest Paperback Publishers by Market Share, 1976

Publisher	Estimated Share
Bantam	20%
Dell	15
CBS (Fawcett-Popular Library)	14
New American Library	10
Ballantine	9
Pocket Books	9
Avon	7
Largest Seven	84%

SOURCE: Knowledge Industry Publications, Inc.

DISTRIBUTION CHANNELS FOR MASS MARKET BOOKS

The predominant mode of distribution of mass market paperbacks is the network of 500-odd independent distributors (IDs), who in turn service the 60,000 to 80,000 retail outlets. Somewhat over half of all mass market books are distributed via IDs. Fawcett does about 60% of its business through IDs; Avon, Bantam, and Pocket Books each about half. AAP figures from nine reporting paperback publishers show that 59% of gross sales were made to wholesalers (IDs) in 1976, compared to 65% in 1973. However, the percentage of net sales made through wholesalers was considerably lower — 52% in 1976 and 57% in 1973. The difference between the percentage of gross and net sales reflects the much higher returns on sales through wholesalers (see the section on returns).

To reach the IDs, most publishers utilize the services of a national distributor, a company that does not take physical possession of books at any time. Rather, the national distributor acts as an intermediary allocating the number of copies of each title that an ID receives and taking care of billing, returns, and other relationships with the IDs. National distributors were originally in the magazine business and added books later on. The books themselves are shipped from publishers' warehouses, according to the instructions of the national distributor. When books arrive at the local independent distributor, they are then broken down into shipments to the ID's retail customers, with some IDs being relatively sophisticated in their determination of who gets what, whereas others put together orders in a more haphazard manner. Returned books filter back through the system, but in most cases the physical copy of the book is destroyed by the ID, with only the cover or an affidavit going back to the national distributor for credit.

A second distribution channel, directly from publisher to retailer, works much as it does with the trade books, but is a less significant proportion of mass market sales because of the vast number of total outlets and the hesitancy of publishers to get involved with small customers. However, a growing area of direct-to-retailer sales is in the relationships to the national bookstore chains, such as Waldenbooks and B. Dalton, which buy in large quantities for all their stores directly from the publishers, as well as to mass merchandising chains such as J.C. Penney.

A third approach, small but expanding, is through paperback jobbers, which include the large jobbers such as Baker & Taylor, Bookazine, and Ingram, all enlarging their paperback offerings, as well as paperback specialists, such as A&A Distributors in Massachusetts and Ray Serguine & Co. of Colorado. Unlike the IDs, who are restricted to a local territory, the jobbers sell throughout the country, shipping by common carrier and mail, to chain stores or local stores that want to centralize all their purchases or are dissatisfied with their local ID.

FORM, FUNCTION OF THE INDEPENDENT DISTRIBUTOR

Independent distributors (who refer to themselves as wholesalers) were traditionally "independent" of the American News Co., a distributing company of newspapers and magazines that had a virtual monopoly in this field in 1900. However, some hearty entrepreneurs challenged that monopoly. Initially, paperback publishers distributed both through American News and the IDs, but over the years the bulk of the business went to IDs through national distributors, as American News de-emphasized and finally terminated its book division. Today, each ID has an exclusive franchise in its territory, although for larger accounts IDs face competition from jobbers and publishers. If a publisher wishes to reach the thousands of small outlets serviced by the local ID on a contract basis, he has little alternative to the ID, even if that ID does not do a very effective job of distributing books.

Although there are over 500 IDs, not all carry books; perhaps only 200 have any significance for paperback sales. In a survey undertaken for the Council for Periodical Distributors Association (CPDA) by the accounting firm of Arthur Young & Co., 82 reporting IDs averaged a sales mix in 1973 of 29% mass market books, 67% magazines, and 4% children's books. The mass market percentage was down from 32% in 1972 and 31% in 1971. The composite figure did not vary significantly in relation to the size of the reporting IDs. For firms with under $500,000 in total sales, the percentage of mass market books was 28%; for firms with annual sales of between $500,000 and $1 million, it was 30%; for those with yearly sales of $1 to $2 million, 28%, and for firms with sales of over $2 million, 29%.

IDs are primarily small businesses, with only 26 out of 82 reporting firms in the survey reporting revenues above $2 million. For this reason, figures reporting profitability would likely be understated vis-à-vis those of a publicly owned firm. Nonetheless, for 1973, the composite net profit for IDs was 3.0% of sales, though the firms doing under $500,000 in business averaged 4.4% compared to 2.5% for those with revenue above $2 million. For the year ending June 30, 1972, the average net income for all wholesaling in the United States was 2.5%, indicating that IDs can be at least as profitable as other wholesaling businesses.

Publishers have mixed feelings about the ID system. On the one hand, these local wholesalers appear to be the only effective way of getting thousands of titles to tens of thousands of outlets quickly, which is just what the publishers need. On the other hand, with several notable exceptions, IDs view themselves as being primarily distributors of magazines; books are still a cumbersome and alien appendage. George Wright, the executive vice-president of CPDA, the IDs' trade association, characterizes the book side of the business as representing "20% of the volume, 50% of the headaches, and 0% of the profit." Nonetheless, the CPDA has been working vigorously to improve the distribution of mass market books and is firmly committed to making this a profitable addition to the IDs' business.

Allocations and orders

The mechanics of distribution are as follows: In an average month, a wholesaler could receive about 400 new titles from the national distributors. An ID is either "force fed," is on a "suggested allocation system," or places his own orders for each title as he sees fit. The smaller and/or least interested IDs are force fed, that is, sent a quantity of each title as determined by the national distributor. The origin of this practice was twofold. First, the IDs could not evaluate each title as it came out — they have neither the inclination nor wherewithal to make this determination. Thus, the national distributor determined the quantity. Second, publishers felt that the only way to get their product onto the retailers' racks was to send out huge quantities — sales of 600 out of 1000 may be better than 400 out of 600. In practice, the system is a nightmare. Many IDs are so overwhelmed with incoming products, set at insanely high levels for each title, that they have sent some orders back unopened. Force feeding, though still in use, is on the decline.

More prevalent is the suggested allocation. A good allocation system is based on a computer model that analyzes which types of books are sold best by different IDs around the country. Thus, a distributor in the Des Moines area may have a formula for Fawcett books under which, in each month, he takes 20% westerns, 25% mysteries, 15% bestsellers, etc. The big and successful IDs can modify the suggested allocation any way they want, in effect establishing their own ordering procedure. Although there may be considerable pressure from the national distributor or publisher to take certain quantities, the decision is ultimately with the ID. Yet IDs still complain that the "suggestions" are wildly inflated, so that they end up merely "unsuggesting" their order to what reality should have dictated in the first place.

Since 1975, the industry sales leader, Bantam Books, has had a policy that no wholesaler, regardless of its size, will be shipped a book it does not order. Others in the industry claim that they have been following a similar policy or are moving toward one. Nonetheless, the problem remains, how will the smaller ID know which titles to order from the hundreds he is confronted with each month?

Once the wholesaler has the books, they must be broken down into allocations for the retailers. Ironically, IDs turn around and force feed most small outlets a monthly diet of new titles. There is not much dispute with the process at this level, since the newsstands or drugstores with a few dozen display pockets depend on the ID for just this function. Most small and medium size IDs send their books to customers along with their magazine distribution. This is done in the form of a "prepack" in which the wholesaler determines the mix of books and quantities that each outlet should receive and prepares a separate bundle for each. The paperback books for all but the smallest accounts are stacked in individual piles, one title to a pile and often arranged by publisher in descending order of price. Each individual dealer's shipment is picked according to a distribution strategy chosen by the ID. In cases where the retailer's book requirements are not large, the book bundles are combined with the magazine bundles on a delivery truck for a single drop. However, most large wholesalers find that many dealers are sufficiently large to warrant a separate delivery schedule for books.

Wholesalers who take the book business most seriously have made use of the book truck approach. Under this system, route drivers are, in effect, mobile warehouses. The driver takes inventory at each account, removing old stock from the racks and replacing these as well as out-of-stock titles that are still moving with supplies from the truck. Book truck operations have the advantage of establishing a contact between the driver and a limited number of dealers on a repetitive basis, with the driver being better able to cater to the unique needs of each customer than a remote book manager making allocations. Nonetheless, it is a more expensive mode than the prepack approach. One compromise has been to have the book truck driver rely on prepacks from the warehouse, but still carry an inventory of best-selling books on the truck to replenish a dealer's depleted stock.

In many instances, the ID's service includes merchandising the books, taking old books from the racks, and filling in the new ones. In other cases, he merely drops off the new bundle and takes back those titles that the dealer has decided he no longer wants. Decisions relating to which books get returned are tied to the number of new books coming in, since outlets have only a fixed number of pockets, whether a 5000 pocket bookstore or a two dozen pocket newsstand. Control is, of necessity, simplistic, Frequently, new books are arranged on the top rows, with older books moving down the rack, until they are removed from the bottom rows. In other cases, dates are stamped on books by the dealer and any remaining copies are returned after a predetermined period.

IDs are most effective in servicing small, nonbookstore outlets, such as newsstands and drugstores. They have been less successful in obtaining the larger accounts, who would rather get the larger discounts offered by the publishers. Small customers get a standard 20% discount, as for magazines. Larger customers qualify for a 30% discount, whereas major bookstore accounts must be offered as much as 40% if the ID wants to compete with jobbers and publishers for their volume. The ID buys books through the national distributor at 46% off list, although in some cases he may qualify for another 1% to 4% off under an incentive program. The incentive is based on a formula combining the return rate and the year-to-year sales increase. However, because the wholesalers depend more on the suggested allocations of the publishers than the jobbers, who order exactly what they want, most IDs do not come out favorably on the return rate and are less likely to qualify for the incentive than the jobbers.

Areas of ID growth

One paperback publisher has been quoted, anonymously, in *Publisher's Weekly* as predicting the end of independent distribution within five years. The whole business will be on a direct to retailer basis. Little in the direction of the mass market industry supports this projection. In fact, numerous cases indicate that the movement may be in just the opposite way. The same arguments that make jobbers a natural course for much of the trade sales holds for the mass market, only more so. It is virtually impossible for publishers to deal with 80,000 retailers, let alone be able to analyze each of their needs. And most retailers, except for the relatively small percentage of outlets that are bookstores, cannot take the time nor develop the expertise to make the selection and watch the inventory of a few dozen or a few hundred book titles.

Moreover, publishers need the IDs to provide the quick access to the market when they want to get a book out fast. The instant extras of Bantam and Dell are examples of books that could never have reached the largest number of outlets in the short time needed to promote their immediacy.

Three distinct avenues of development are encouraging to the vitality of independent distributors as a major link in the paperback book distribution channel, with the result that more total books may be sold to more people with greater efficiency.

1.   The increased willingness of publishers to let IDs do their own buying. Although small IDs may never have the inclination for this task, those that account for most of the business will. New American Library, for example, estimates that fewer than 40% of the IDs account for 84% of its sales. In doing their own ordering, the wholesalers will find they can lower their inventory and most certainly reduce the return problem and hence increase their efficiency.

2.   Growth in chain store sales. The CPDA has been working aggressively in this area. Mass market paperbacks need to be sold where people are, and the chain stores, whether K-Mart, Sears, or Safeway, are where the customers can be reached. The CPDA has been pushing the Family Reading Center concept, a distinct department within the chain store, serviced by the ID, carrying magazines and mass market books. The economics for the establishment of book and magazine displays are weighted heavily in favor of the publishers. IDs can show, for example, that a combined paperback book/magazine display can return $7 to $11 per dollar of inventory investment, compared to an overall average of $3.95 per dollar in supermarkets and $7.40 for convenience stores.

The penetration of paperback books, via the Family Reading Center concept, has the potential for staggering proportions. The Magazine & Paperback Marketing Institute, via a questionnaire to wholesalers, estimates that there are about 10,000 of these centers already placed. As a conservative guess, they have created an additional space for 960,000 pockets and as many as 5 million books, representing a paperback inventory of perhaps $6.5 million. At a normal ten times inventory turnover, this represents as much as $65 million worth of paperback book business in chain food stores alone. Projecting this to future growth, this one area may generate $135 to $180 million in retail sales. Already, paperback book and magazine sales account for about 2.7% of total supermarket sales, more than the percentage of cookies, crackers, eggs, ice cream, or frozen foods. (See the profile of Charles Levy for a case study of one ID's experience with chain store sales.)

In this regard, however, it is crucial that the book publishers not hesitate in applying the Universal Product Code to their book covers. It is unlikely that supermarkets will want to carry any volume product that is not compatible with the very expensive scanning and computer devices that will enable them to reduce their handling and labor costs substantially. Up to now, publishers have resisted including the unsightly bar codes, largely at the insistence of the art directors. But the payback in additional books sold by gaining supermarket display, as well as the additional convenience that wholesalers and publishers will gain in being able to scan returns, far outweigh such considerations.

3. Improved data processing and allocation systems. The CPDA has given high priority to the development of a system that could help IDs in making allocation decisions to outlets that would optimize sales while minimizing returns, yet be simple, inexpensive and practical for a large number of IDs. To date, only bits and pieces of the proposed system have been implemented by a few IDs. Essentially, the system would define each book by one of ten or so categories, such as romance, westerns, mystery, science fiction, and the like. The goal would be the ability of each ID to be able to make purchase decisions based on the performance of each publisher's line in each category. Allocations to retail stores would be based on similar historical sales figures.

Typical of the level of achievement in implementation is the information output of United News, a $30 million ID in the Philadelphia area. United News has established categories and can now analyze each outlet's sales by categories, in much the same way that many publishers and national distributors can tell what each of the IDs are selling. A more complete automated information and allocation system has been implemented by the Charles Levy Circulating Co. and its Computer Book Service (CBS) subsidiary. (See the profile, Chapter XIV.) Levy/CBS is the independent distributor in Chicago and has become the largest mass market paperback wholesaler and jobber in the country, increasing its mass market paperback sales from $9.5 million in 1972 to an estimated $16.7 million in 1975. Its commitment to paperbacks, aggressiveness in marketing, and investment in computer information lie behind this expansion, which is not unlike Ingram's growth.

RETURNS

Books returned from the retailer to the ID or jobber and thereon to the publisher are even a greater source of concern than in the trade end of the business. The 1974 CPDA survey of 71 wholesalers reported that a record 45.7% of all mass market paperback books shipped to IDs were returned, compared to the 1974 figure for 11 publishers reporting to the AAP of 36.3%. The lower publisher returns reflect the fact that jobbers and stores that buy direct and are not force fed or on an allocation system control returns better.

As in trade books, returns cost everyone money. But there are several differences in the mass market paperback category. First, the books themselves are rarely returned. This practice dates back to when paperbacks cost $.25 and $.35, and the cost of handling and shipping returned books was greater than printing new ones. Second, paperbacks do not hold up as well on the newsstands or racks as hardcover books, so that they often cannot be reshipped anyway. Taking a page from the magazine industry, IDs merely "strip" the front covers from the books and return them sorted by price, destroying the books themselves. The national distributors give the IDs credit on the returned copies, just as a publisher provides credit to a direct account. Finally, many paperbacks have unusually short shelf lives — some say as brief as a week, although 30 days would be more realistic. It would be far more efficient for IDs themselves to call in titles that are not moving well at some locations and reship them to outlets that need more rather than to just pull in what hasn't sold and strip the covers. Some things are changing, however. As the cover price of many mass market books edges up to $1.95 and beyond, it is more likely that publishers will demand that certain paperback books be returned *in toto*, the economics making it more advantageous than adding further printings. This is especially true with books that catch on in different parts of the country in a wavelike fashion, so that as a title dies here, unsold books are reshipped elsewhere. The problem is how to treat the inevitably returned group of unsalable books, dogeared from handling or otherwise.

Reasons for returns

Why are returns so great a proportion of the total books shipped? Answers vary, depending on what segment of the industry is responding. Retailers claim there are too many new titles being issued. IDs complain that they are forced to take books they don't want. Even under the suggested allocation program, IDs often find that they must take the bottom end of a publisher's line in order to get the better books. Publishers frequently respond that IDs are more oriented toward their magazine business, don't understand or care about books, and are not very efficient or aggressive in selling them.

However, the most responsible solution is one that is agreed on by the more thoughtful leaders in the industry. Sidney Stern, president of Philadelphia's United News, echoes the philosophy of Bantam head Oscar Dystel when he says that the lines with the best titles and ordering procedures have the lowest returns. The result is a cycle that breeds success. For example, by having a strong selling line, as well as a national distributor (Select), which has worked closely with the IDs as a separate book division, IDs have learned to trust Bantam and to accept its allocations. Notes one influential executive on the wholesalers' end: "The middle of Bantam's line is better than the top of others."

Along with considerable editorial foresight, Bantam has been a conservative publisher. It establishes relatively low initial print orders, sprinkling the books around the country and using the vast Select network, as well as its own field force of 60, to get a quick feedback on how well books are selling and in what parts of the country. If the results are favorable, then Bantam will push reorders and go back for additional printings. Even a sure-fire seller such as *Jaws* had an initial print order of "only" 1.5 million.

Four months later, a total of 4.5 million were in print. As the cost of printing and handling becomes greater, such a conservative approach will likely become more prevalent in the industry as an alternative to accepting high returns.

Besides having a good list and a conservative printing philosophy, a publisher can help reduce returns through an efficient organization to handle reorders. Jobbers, IDs, and retailers all know that Bantam, among a few others, can get reorders filled fast. Thus, they are less tempted to overorder initially, helping Bantam spread its stock over a wider territory. "It is the publisher with the poorer titles, the less sophistication in reordering, that forces the larger orders," explains United News's Stern.

Returns by publishers

Table VII-2 gives evidence that the industry's return problem should be restated to indicate that the problem lies with certain book lines and distributors more than others. Thus, whereas Bantam, with the most books in the marketplace, had returns through wholesalers of under 33%, Curtis had returned an astounding 78%, and Warner, a major publisher with a weak backlist, had returns approaching 50%. Success in controlling returns is not limited to large publishers. The overall leader in sales to draw is small Harlequin Books. Harlequin's publishing philosophy offers an interesting contrast to that of other paperback publishers, since all of its books are in the category of women's romances, all employ the same cover design, and carry much lower prices ($.75 and $.95) than the typical paperback title. This combination, says Harlequin, has enabled it to build brand identification among consumers, who often buy two or three titles at a time, and to keep returns low.

SETTING PRINT ORDERS

A corollary to the specter of returns is the iffy process by which publishers set print orders for their new titles. At its best, it is a combination of art and science; at the worst, a wild guess. The difficulty of setting print orders, whether for trade or mass market, relates back to the unique property of a book. Unlike a

TABLE VII-2:   Mass Market Paperback Book Returns Through Independent Distributors, 1974

National Distributor Book Line	Returns as % of Draw	Sales as % Total Retain Volume
Capital total	56.8	1.3
Midwood Books	47.0	0.7
Belmont Tower	63.1	0.4
Curtis total	78.3	0.8
Dell Total	43.0	11.0
Fawcett total	43.0	11.7
IND-Warner total	49.0	5.4
ICD total	50.3	12.3
Avon	42.5	7.0
Pyramid	51.6	2.0
Popular Library	60.0	3.0
Kable total	49.6	5.4
Berkley	49.3	2.6
Beeline	50.7	1.3
NAL total	50.3	10.7
Signet	50.6	8.3
Mentor	10.5	0.5
Daw/Tiger Beat	60.0	0.3
Award	58.6	0.7
Pocket Books - Ace total	43.9	13.1
Pocket Books	44.5	8.0
Ace	56.6	1.9
Harlequin	31.1	2.1
Playboy Press	62.6	0.3
PDC total	49.8	6.2
Ballantine	48.8	5.1
Beagle	59.3	0.4
SELECT - Bantam total	32.4	18.9
GRAND total	45.7	99.3[1]

[1] Misc. book lines not included in table added to total

SOURCE: Council for Periodical Distributors Associations.

magazine, with a base of subscriptions and a history of sales, and unlike a new brand of toothpaste, which has a measurable, known total market and characteristics, each new book title is a new product, with no history. For sure, there is a history of sales for other books in that category by the publisher and possibly for the author. Thus, there is some experience that may be parlayed into a feel for the right figure.

But public taste is volatile and there is always the problem of what new books in the same category the competition will be offering the same month. A title tied in to the release of a movie may die if the movie is delayed or, worse, is itself a failure. Effective cover art is undeniably an aid in paperback sales, but there are too many books being published and limited budgets that make prior market research unrealistic. At best, two or three alternative covers will be shown to the field salesmen, who will use their best judgment to provide input on which is the most salable. And though publishers deny any exact correlation, the size of the advance paid for reprint rights obviously influences the print order. A paperback house that lays out $1 million for a block-buster hardcover title and sets an initial advertising and promotion budget of $100,000 knows that it must sell upward of 1.4 million copies at $1.95 just to break even.

Certainly how well the hardcover version sold helps provide an index in setting the order for a reprint title. Moving more into science, those publishers who have developed computer-based systems for analyzing sales and returns by categories and IDs have at least a starting point for establishing likely orders from the 50% of their sales that move through the IDs. The final print order is thus a melding of considerations within the framework of the publishing philosophy of the house. The same considerations that will yield an initial order of 400,000 for one publisher might result in a smaller order from a more conservative house such as Bantam.

ECONOMIC AND DYNAMIC FACTORS IN MASS MARKET PAPERBACKS

Although "mass market" is still the term that applies to those books that are distributed through IDs to a mass audience, these paperback books do not constitute the monolithic market they once were. First of all, the market for these books has broadened and diversified, becoming in the process more specialized. There are not only the bestseller reprints but also the rising tide of original paperbacks. Besides the gothics and westerns aimed at the bus terminal newsstand market, there are how-to books such as *A Guide to Filmmaking* and the instant books such as the White House transcripts. Some mass market books are prepared very much with the school and college market in mind and it is not unusual to have different covers on a title depending on its intended audience. From its early days as primarily an entertainment medium, paperbacks now cover the spectrum from sex to science.

New ventures and distribution patterns

The latest trend is the movement of paperback publishers into what is called the large-format or quality paperback field. This involves publishing large-size books on better paper stock, often containing extensive art or photographs, and carrying a price tag closer to hardcover trade books than to rack-sized paperbacks. Examples are Avon's edition of *The Best of Life*, various titles from Ballantine, Bantam's edition of William Manchester's *The Glory and the Dream* and its *The Compleat Astrologer*.

At the same time, the patterns of distribution have broadened. Besides the normal mass market channels, the trade book jobbers have come to realize that they need these books to have a complete line and provide a full service for their customers. Retailers, who have traditionally reserved separate sections of their store for mass market paperbacks, are now looking at integrating hardcover and softcover books into a unified display, with none other than old-line Brentano's among the leaders. This accords the mass market books a recognition as a respectable publishing format. The book review media are slowly recognizing this trend in giving paperbacks more visibility.

Consistent with this new-found status, leaders in paperback publishing, such as Avon and Bantam, have stopped seeing themselves as the junior partners in the publishing pyramid. In fact, it has been their purchases of reprint rights in recent years that have kept many hardback publishers alive. As shown in Table II-5, it is the "other publishing income," largely subsidiary rights from the paperback publishers, that kept the proverbial wolf from the door. As such, the mass market publishers see no reason why they must wait to bid for limited-term licenses from hardcover houses. Instead, many are pioneering a field of "co-publishing" joint ventures, whereby the paper publisher may acquire initial rights and offer the work to a hardcover house, the trade paper rights to perhaps another firm, and then publish the mass market edition later, with film, book club, and other subsidiary rights sold to the extent practical. The implications of this for the publishing industry are sizable, for they add to the leverage of the entire industry. But they also provoke a need for multiple approaches to distribution and marketing, since the "normal" channel distribution loses significance in the dynamic climate.

Growth rates and profit margins

Economically, the mass market paperback field appears to be entering a period of some difficulty. Its very high growth rate throughout the 1960s and early 1970s permitted paperback publishers to absorb hefty increases in the amounts laid out for advances, as well as hikes in paper and manufacturing costs. In 1974, when the industry sales rose by a meager 2.9%, profits were squeezed. Of publishers reporting to AAP's operating survey, 10 mass market houses reported average pretax profits of 3.9%, a sharp dip from the 8.6% in 1973. Margins did not rebound until 1976, but at 6.1%, they have room for further improvement.

Moreover, profits are heavily skewed by size of company, with the four largest publishers in 1974 reporting average pretax profits of 8.6%, whereas the six smaller ones had an average loss of 6.7%. Actually, the situation is probably even more dramatic. Though Bantam has under a quarter of the industry sales volume, it very likely earns more than half and maybe as much as two-thirds of the industry profits, given losses at some companies.

In addition, the paperback houses face ticklish decisions as the price of paperbacks goes up. Whereas traditional pricing formulas would call for pricing more and more books at over $2, publishers have been hesitant to break this barrier except for major titles because of their fears of consumer resistance.

The push to broaden distribution and to publish large-format or quality paperbacks can be seen as a reaction to tightening market conditions in the mass market field. And, as rights auctions escalate, paperback publishers will have no choice but to be involved in major books from their inception, acquiring paperback rights directly from the author, engaging in co-publishing deals with trade houses, or forming their own hardcover imprints, as Dell and Pocket Books have done. Eventually there may be a shakeout as some of the weaker companies are forced out of business, but in the near term the market is becoming more competitive, not less so. New American Library has become a more aggressive factor and has regained its market share; Pocket Books is showing renewed vitality as the result of an infusion of capital from conglomerate Gulf + Western, which acquired Pocket's parent, Simon and Schuster, in 1975; Warner Paperback Library continues to pursue a strategy of expensive television advertising and of movie tie-ins with the Warner Brothers motion-picture studio; and Ballantine is going after more big books since its acquisition by RCA/Random House. Popular Library, the CBS subsidiary, remains a minor factor in the industry, but the addition of Fawcett gives CBS a strong position in the mass market field.

CONCLUSIONS AND A LOOK AT THE FUTURE

Although mass market publishers are experimenting with more original titles, or with buying first rights and selling trade houses the hardcover rights, the nature of the distribution will also be subject to experimentation and innovation. Among the likely new directions are the following:

- ID ownership of retail bookstores. The more aggressive IDs are entering the retail field with the objective of adding to profits, of course, but also to get a better feel for the retail market, in effect, on the job market research. The stores also can be used as a showplace to provide other retail bookstore customers with tips on improved operations. United News has seven suburban Book of Knowledge outlets, Charles Levy runs the Book Market, Suits News in Detroit is also in the bookstore business. In all, IDs run over 600 bookstores and the trend is for more.

● Greater control over purchasing and allocations. The key to book allocation is in buying. Clearly, publishers are giving greater leeway to IDs to determine for themselves what categories of books sell best in their locale. Some publishers, Fawcett among them, can help by providing detailed category and title histories for each ID served. At the ID end, more publishers will gather the category information that will allow them to distribute books to outlets in a mix that will increase sales and reduce returns.

● More sales to chain stores. Charles Levy's Computer Book Service has shown that chain operations can be convinced that dealing with a full-service jobber/distributor can be more advantageous than trying to do it all themselves. The gross margin is not nearly as important as the net, and operations as sophisticated as J.C. Penney's and Sears have no doubt done the analysis and decided that the smaller gross discount still yields a greater bottom line for their book departments. Other IDs can make the same points to regional or local chain stores, thus adding major large accounts to supplement their traditional newsstand, small drugstore strongholds. Supermarket and drug chains are incorporating the Family Reading Center concept in a program with a great potential.

● Fewer IDs. There has been a slow, steady thinning out of IDs, which, to an extent is a positive trend since the large number of small IDs made efficiencies less feasible and the addition of EDP controls more difficult. The one real distributing chain in the field is ARA Services, a Los Angeles based vending and catering firm that owns about 22 formerly independent wholesalers in such places as Milwaukee, Los Angeles, and San Francisco. ARA accounts for an estimated 10%-15% of all paperback books distributed by IDs. Although a Federal Trade Commission consent decree has stymied ARA's expansion in this field, it is likely that several other small chains of IDs will be created through mergers and acquisitions over the next decade.

● A reduction in the rapid escalation in cover prices. The main reasons are perceived price resistance from consumers and the overall easing of costs, especially in paper. Since 1967, mass market book price increases have slightly exceeded those of hardcover books and greatly surpassed the overall climb in consumer prices. Right now, $1.95 is the most popular price, although more major titles have shown the ability to stand a $2.25 or higher cover. More likely will be the closing of ranks, with the gradual elimination of the $.95 book. But the mass market book remains a good buy, compared to prices for magazines (most now over $1), a movie ticket, or a record album.

● Emphasis on sales to schools (discussed in Chapter XI). The market is largely virgin territory for those IDs or jobbers who want to pursue it. This could be in the form of book fairs, library supply, or the use of paperbacks in classrooms as supplements and alternatives to texts.

● Slow progress toward better industry-wide information systems. A certain amount of coordination among the larger retailers, the IDs, and the publishers would enable greater progress to be made industry-wide, but the prospects are not encouraging. For example, in planning for a system to provide category distribution and sales analysis, the CPDA has established seven "standard" categories. But the Charles Levy/CBS system uses 13 categories and Dell has 15. Before long, the advantages of the data will be overcome by the lack of a common interface, making ordering, distribution and analysis as confusing as ever.

VIII

Getting Books to the Reader:
Books Clubs and Mail Order Publications

Since 1971, the first year that mail order publications were tallied as a separate category by the AAP, combined book club and mail order sales of books have held steady as a portion of total book sales, edging from 14.5% in 1971 to 15.1% in 1973 and up to 16.5% of the market in 1976. What relative growth there has been in these categories has been contributed mainly by mail order books, which represent 8.3% of sales, compared to 6.7% in 1971. In dollar amounts, Table III-2 lists book club sales at $343.1 million, an increase of 49% since 1971, whereas the mail order category experienced a stronger growth of 79% to 349.9 million in 1976.

Book clubs and mail order selling represent the response of publishers and marketers to the dearth of good bookstore outlets throughout much of the country. Initially, these direct-to-the-consumer channels concentrated on selling general interest books, but in recent years, much of the growth has been in special interest clubs and series. Their primary tools in reaching potential customers are mass advertising and direct mail solicitations. Their emphasis has generally been on a high volume of sales at low cost per unit and tight per unit margins. In effect, the operations take the dollars saved in retailer discounts and apply them to advertising, mailing costs, and a somewhat lower list price.

BOOK CLUBS

The Book-of-the-Month Club, acquired by Time Inc. in 1977, pioneered the book club idea in the United States, and was immediately successful following its start in 1926. The Literary Guild imitated the Book-of-the-Month Club shortly thereafter, also with success. Today, there are about 130 book clubs, most of them small and catering to special interests. Twenty of these clubs are run by publishing giant Doubleday. Literary Guild (owned by Doubleday) is now the leader, with approximately 1.7 million members to BOMC's 1.5 million. The growth of the BOMC has been slow in recent years, whereas LG has more than doubled its membership since 1970. In the late 1960s and early 1970s, a number of magazine publishers saw a book club as a natural extension of their subscriber mailing lists and a veritable express-way to fat profits. But time has proven otherwise, with many of these ventures collapsing or stalling along the way.

Those clubs with the know-how, investment, and forebearance have made this mode of book sales pay off. In fiscal 1977, BOMC showed a net profit of 7.7%, earning $4.9 million on revenues of $64.6 million, although down from its previous year's sales and profit figures. Other book clubs either bury their figures in corporate summaries or are privately held. However, Knowledge Industry Publications has estimated that Doubleday's total book club operation had revenues of over $100 million.

On the other hand, the highly touted (in 1972) Saturday Review Book Club faded when the magazine went sour. Time Inc. dropped a small bundle before shutting down the Book Find Club and letting BOMC take over the Fortune and Sports Illustrated Book Clubs. Playboy, after some heady growth, claims that the membership of its book club has stabilized at 150,000 with sales of $8-$10 million. Whether the club is making money must be viewed with some skepticism in light of the company's overall troubles.

Among the larger special interest clubs, Times Mirror's Outdoor Life, Popular Science, and Woman's How-To clubs have boosted their sales about 25% between 1971 and 1974, to $15 million, but here again, membership has been at a flat 500,000 total. Meredith's Better Homes and Gardens Family Book Service has been static, but it is gaining members for the newer crafts club. Macmillan, Prentice-Hall, and McGraw-Hill all have professionally oriented book clubs that appear to be prospering. Revenues at Macmillan are in the $18-$22 million range; Prentice-Hall's clubs do about $7 million; and McGraw-Hill's clubs have yearly sales of $3-$4 million.

BOOK CLUB OPERATIONS AND ECONOMICS

Book clubs are marketers, not publishers of books (though there are gray areas — Prentice-Hall's clubs sell only its own books, Literary Guild creates books specially for its members). In their most stripped down form, the book clubs offer new members an attractive incentive for joining, frequently along with the requirement that they purchase a certain number of books during their membership or within a given period of time. After that, some clubs require that members purchase a small number of books to remain on the active list. Following the fulfillment of the minimum purchase, members are free to quit. Most of the clubs offer their books at a price below list price.

Club advantages

The major selling points of the clubs are:

• The initial joining package. BOMC and the Literary Guild offer four bestsellers, chosen from a field of 50 or more, all for $1. This come-on is highly alluring compared to the list price of $7.95 to $20.00 per book or set.

• The convenience and service. Faced with a multitude of new books, people interested in buying books can look to the clubs for guidance in their selections and alternates. For people who live in areas that do not have bookstores that carry all these titles (especially in special interest or professional fields), it may save much time and aggravation.

• Lower price than list. The method of savings varies: some clubs, such as the Literary Guild, offer all their selections at substantial discounts. Others, such as BOMC, emphasize discounts less but provide for bonus plans, whereby each regular purchase gains a credit toward the purchase of a dividend at perhaps 70% off list price from a special selection of books. (Although by the time postage and handling costs are added, the savings may not be so substantial).

Yet the creeping overall growth rate in book club memberships indicate that there is still resistance to the club concept. These focus on two related fears:

• The initial membership "obligates" the buyer to spending more in the form of the agreement to purchase a minimum number of books.

• The "negative option" cycle. This is the almost universal procedure by which members are sent the club's selection automatically — unless the member returns a card informing the club to send an alternate or no book at all. In the past, there had been abuse of the negative option by the club operators, but under duress from the Federal Trade Commission they have cleaned up the source of many complaints, such as not allowing enough time between sending the notice and shipping the book. BOMC, for instance, gives 25 to 30 days' notice. Still, once the book is sent, the customer is obligated to pay and many people do not want to have to be always alert to sending back the card for offerings they do not desire.

Marketing and acquisition costs and strategies

The key to a successful book club is to acquire members at as low a price as possible and to keep them buying books for as long as possible. It is this combination of cost of acquisition and activity that determines profitability. Thus, BOMC claims that it has been able to increase sales and profit despite a flat membership because it is replacing infrequent buying members with more active ones. Having to replace, on the average, 40% of its membership each year, BOMC needs 50,000 *new* members each year just to stay even.

Finding the best places to get new members is one of the fine arts of book club sales. "If you bring in the wrong person, it hurts the club," warns Ed Fitzgerald, president of BOMC. To get its members, BOMC spent $9.5 million in 1974, Doubleday at least as much. Over the years, the major clubs have learned much about direct mail and advertising, but different approaches are appropriate for clubs with varying resources and needs. The clubs tied to magazines can often use the subscriber lists as well as preferential rates for advertisements in the company's magazines. The independent clubs must buy space like any other advertiser and rent mailing lists, although the older ones acquire extensive in-house lists over the years. Reader's Digest's Condensed Book Club, which offers only four volumes a year, each with four to six condensed bestsellers, is marketed largely to RD's own subscriber list.

For the larger and general interest clubs, the bulk of the advertising budget goes into the mass media. However, BOMC has cut down its media allocation in recent years from 70% to 60%, increasing its direct mail budget by the difference. The Literary Guild has placed greater emphasis on direct mail all along. Right now, BOMC is finding that members acquired via direct mail solicitations "buy more and pay better" than those coming in from mass media sources.

Conforming to previously noted findings that book buyers are largely college-educated, mailing lists used by clubs are purchased from "upscale" magazines, with BOMC using *Horizon, Country Journal, New Times, Apartment Life, Time,* and *Newsweek,* among others. BOMC also buys a list of *Cosmopolitan* expirations. Another avenue of pursuit used by clubs are lists of those who have previously shown a willingness to purchase books by mail. Thus, customers of the Time-Life continuity series books ("The Old West," "Art of Sewing," et al.) make appropriate prospects, as do those who have bought single titles from Simon and Schuster's active coupon advertisements in the media.

The cost of acquisition ultimately depends on how good the mailing list that was used. Based on a total cost of $24,000 for a 100,000 piece mailing, a positive return of 2% would mean an up-front expense of $12 per member. About $15 is the highest any club would consider even marginally acceptable. A return of 6% is about as good as could ever be expected, or a cost of $4 each. The "average" new member (including one brought in from media advertising), costs about $11-$12.

Display advertising works in a similar manner. BOMC buys "as much space as we can" in the *New York Times Book Review* section, as well as the *Times Magazine,* competing in the former with the Literary Guild for the back cover. *New York Review of Books,* the literary magazines (*Harper's,* etc.), the news magazines, and occasionally the women's magazines are the logical sources for the general interest clubs. The special interest clubs would, of course, go into magazines endemic to their subject matter. The cost of the *Times Book Review* back cover is a minimum of about $4500, meaning that only 450 responses (from a circulation of 1.4 million) would bring the cost to $10 per member.

The Guild and BOMC are the only two clubs that could occasionally take advantage of more eye-catching color inserts in Sunday newspapers, since the cost of stuffing the insert in *The Times* is over $20,000. This would be an alternative to sending a brochure of similar printing cost via direct mail, at a postage cost of over $61,000 to a similar size, albeit more highly selected, audience. (The Guild has also experimented a fair amount with television, but has not found a way to make it pay.)

Added to the acquisition cost is the expense of providing the premium for joining. Although many of the smaller or professional clubs are not as generous as BOMC and the Literary Guild, the effect is similar. The cost to BOMC is an average of $6, including manufacturing cost plus a reduced royalty to publisher and author. For this, the income is $1. In all cases, postage and handling costs are passed on to the client. The book club has now spent $16 or more, with a revenue of $1.

But now, the powerful attraction of book club economics. In the next year, the member purchases at least four books, at an average of $8 each. Shipping and handling costs are passed through, so these need not be considered here. The clubs are responsible for their own separate printings, but manufacturing cost, based on long runs and volume contracts with suppliers, may be as low as $1.10 per book. To this is added a royalty of 10% of the club price, for a direct cost of $1.90, or $7.60 to fulfill the four books. The resulting income statement is shown in Table VIII-1.

BOMC has small additional direct expenses, such as sending the book club announcements 15 times a year. The Literary Guild has a mailing every 26 days or 14 a year. It also has to defray its general overhead, including the massive automated processing center in Camp Hill, Pennsylvania. Thus, in the first year it is likely that, using these assumptions, the club would get back its cash investment and make some contribution to profit and overhead, though not much. But this is where the quality of the member comes in. Many customers quit at this point, or even

TABLE VIII-1:   Book Club Economics, Year 1

		Per Member
Revenue from four books		$32.00
Revenue from premium		1.00
Total revenue, first year		33.00
Less:		
Acquisition cost	$12.00	
Initial fulfillment	6.00	
First year fulfillment	7.60	
		$25.60
Gross profit		$ 7.40

worse, keep getting the announcements but return the cards refusing any shipments. These people will have their membership terminated after a year. The average member, however, stays in for two years. If in the second year, the member purchases three books, the reward to the club becomes evident, as illustrated by Table VIII-2.

Thus, over two years, the club's gross profit will come to $25.70 on a total revenue of $57. BOMC club dividend books are priced to cover manufacturing costs and royalties, so the regular selections must carry all of the overhead.

The economics for each club would differ slightly. Literary Guild, for example, might spread out its average membership (and expense) over a longer time by not putting a time limit on fulfilling the four book minimum. The Library of Contemporary Education gives members two years to buy three books.

TABLE VIII-2:   Book Club Economics, Year 2

	Per Member
Revenue:	
3 x $8@	$24.00
Expense:	
3 x $1.90@	5.70
Gross profit	$18.30

Industry figures reported to AAP must be regarded with caution, because clubs vary so greatly in size and operating policies. Nevertheless, of 66 clubs with net sales of $239.8 million reporting to AAP in 1976, advertising and promotion costs averaged 33.5% of sales. Assuming an average membership life of two years, the direct cost of advertising and promotion to acquire new members, shown in Tables VIII-1 and VIII-2, is equal to 31% of those members' purchases. Adding a few dollars for the cost of advertising and promotion to existing members through the announcement bulletins puts the total marketing costs in the 34%-35% range, which is in line with the AAP numbers.

According to the AAP survey, this advertising and promotion cost is the largest chunk of book club expense: manufacturing costs are 25.5% of sales, royalties are 5.8%, fulfillment costs are 9.3%, and general and administrative costs are 18.0%. (Note that the term fulfillment in Tables VIII-1 and VIII-2 refers to the manufacturing and royalty costs of books sent, and disregards the overhead fulfillment costs relating to data processing, list storage, administrative costs, and the like.)

THE ROLE OF CLUBS IN THE INDUSTRY

The book club is a logical channel within the book distribution system, more so in light of the gaping holes in the network of bookstores around the country. When they first started, there was a considerable tide of resentment against them from the bookseller world, complaints that they took sales away from the retail merchants with their low prices and "freebies." But over the years the friction has subsided, to the point where some booksellers will grudgingly admit that book clubs may in fact help sales.

First, there is the prestige and added publicity that comes when a title is chosen as a book club selection or alternate. The club advertisements feature the books, so that those who are not members or will not join for the reasons noted earlier can still use the club's choices as guides through the book maze. Publishers will frequently change their promotion plans if a book has been chosen by a club. The classic example is the story of *The Guns of August*. Macmillan initially published an edition of 3000 — the salesmen thought a book about World War I would be a bore. Then, BOMC picked it as a full selection and overnight the publisher increased its print order to a reported 25,000 and began expanding the advertising budget. Holt, Rinehart, and Winston tripled the print run (and changed the original title) of Joan Haislip's *The Crown of Mexico*, and Norton extended printings of *The Nixon Recession Caper* and Bill Mauldin's *The Brass Ring* after BOMC chose them several years ago.

Book clubs also extend the market for books. This is especially true of the special interest clubs, which promote books that are not the bestseller types and would not often be found in bookstores, except on special order. They also raise book buying consciousness. The sports enthusiast who may not be a regular book buyer could nonetheless be attracted to the Sports Illustrated Book Club, which sells books that would otherwise not have been sold.

Finally, book club advances, from the $85,000 or more that the big ones offer to the few thousand dollars of a minor club, add to the hardcover publishers' income, helping to cover the red ink that might otherwise flow. At the least, by providing extra income for a title that may not have turned a healthy profit on its own, the clubs make it more feasible for the publisher to support books that might otherwise not get published. Publishers are united in their opinion that the selection by a club, especially BOMC, definitely helps trade sales as well as providing a psychological boost.

Possibly the greatest threat to the clubs has been the bookstore chains, Waldenbooks and B. Dalton's They are aggressive merchandisers that are not afraid to discount. Moreover, the chains are moving into areas of the country where there had not been stores before, thus possibly infringing on the book club strongholds. But, although admitting that they will be "tough competition," BOMC, for one, is not overly concerned. BOMC membership is scattered throughout the population, and although they will not release precise breakdowns, BOMC executives claim that BOMC members are concentrated in big cities and in New York and California — the current strongholds of bookstores as well. The general clubs surmise that they can compete effectively with their incentive package at joining, as well as their guidance function in selection. And the chains still do not carry the breadth of special interest selections offered by those smaller clubs.

AVENUES FOR EXPANSION

There are today, at best estimate, 6.7 to 7.2 million book club members, only about 6% of the 1976 population 25 years old or more, but perhaps 50% of the college educated adult population (BOMC claims its membership is 80% college graduates). In terms of absolute numbers, there is no reason to project a growth any greater than a slow upward movement, reflecting the increased educational attainment of the population.

What then are the prospects for this book outlet? One approach is that taken by BOMC — put less emphasis on gross numbers of members and more on the total number of books sold. By further refining their recruitment processes, the clubs can obtain better quality — members who stay active longer and buy more books after fulfilling the initial commitment.

Another approach is to use the club membership as a springboard for selling other merchandise — an approach disdained by BOMC, but implemented with increasing effectiveness at the Doubleday clubs. There, sales of nonbook merchandise are already around 10% of book club revenues. Far more than BOMC, Doubleday has also pushed the special interest clubs with such ventures as the Cook Book (225,000 members), Science Fiction (155,000), and American Garden Guild (120,000) — though it is doubtful that these clubs contribute to profits in anywhere near their proportion of total membership.

What the industry is still awaiting, however, is a true remainder book club, offering the impressive "coffee table" art and picture books and other overstocks and reprints that have become a major ingredient in the sales mix in many retail bookstores.

Doubleday, however, has experimented with a new method for reaching women readers, using that all-purpose solution to every marketer's needs, the supermarket, in an attempt to get to readers directly. Details have been sketchy, but in a pilot program in the Washington, D.C., area, Doubleday had set up displays, offering Guild editions (but at an age when they are ready for the Bargain Club), at $.99. From there, it hoped to entice the buyers into a simple club and from that point use the newly acquired names to build membership in the other clubs. The idea of meeting the shoppers on their home turf sounded promising, especially when adding a book to an already loaded shopping cart does not involve as visible an expense. It also gives the "hands on" feeling of a bookstore, yet reaches numerous people who do not live near or do not by habit frequent bookstores. However, the idea was apparently dropped, since it has not been expanded since that 1975 trial.

Although the general interest book club market may be saturated, there is still opportunity for planned expansion in the theme clubs. Limitations here involve the depth of the editorial material coming out in the specialized field and the breadth of the potential membership. The Hang-Gliding Book Club may not yet be an idea whose time has come, despite a hard core of potential members. The special interest magazines are obviously in the most advantageous position to introduce these, but given the experience of the early 1970s, they must be prepared for an expensive period of buildup. More importantly, their service must meet a genuine need: the proposed club must offer not just an attractive premium, but has to provide books that are currently unavailable through bookstores or regularly in other clubs.

A paperback club

BOMC has moved in a totally different direction, one that the industry will no doubt be watching with vested interest. In launching its Quality Paperback Book Service, BOMC was treading on virgin territory. Paperback book clubs offering the mass market variety have not been very successful because of the low unit cost of the books and consequently, the small margins on orders by members. But QPBS is banking that the larger size, higher quality, higher priced trade paperbacks will carve out a new niche in the book club market, just as many publishers expect a bright future for trade paperbacks generally.

The terms for joining QPBS are stricter than BOMC: the new member is offered three books, at $1 each. Then, the commitment is for six books over the next year. So far, the selections have been mostly backlist titles, since few current books have been published in a trade edition. BOMC has been working to change that, having offered, exclusively for QPBS, a trade edition of Erica Jong's *Fear of Flying* among others. It did the same with E.L. Doctorow's *Ragtime*, published by Random House, which came out in trade for the Quality Club at the same time as the hardcover – and before the mass market edition.

The club's membership was 100,000 by 1977 (having been launched on an experimental scale in January 1974). So far, it is a very intellectual audience, judging from the selections of Joyce, Durrell, and Kafka that are favored. Such a showing is impressive and bodes well for the future of this format, since it is this class of book buyer that must "buy" the idea of the trade paperback as having the same feel and prestige of a hardcover book.

BOMC's commitment should also sharpen the dispute over the status of trade paperback rights, now a source of dispute between hardcover and mass market paperback publishers. Hardcover publishers sensing new markets for higher priced paperbacks will fight to retain rights to this format; mass market houses, seeing new competition for their less expensive editions, will seek to buy all nonhardcover rights. Still, to retain these rights, hardcover publishers will have to demonstrate the courage of their convictions, which means a willingness to issue hardcover and paper editions nearly simultaneously, to the likely detriment of the cloth version.

Quality Paperback Service involves a substantial risk. The average price of the trade paperbacks is about $5.50, yet with typical printings of 500 to 25,000 copies, the manufacturing cost of these books is not too different from hardbacks. QPBS has likely just achieved the membership of over 100,000 to effect the economies needed for an acceptable profit.

MAIL ORDER

Mail order sales really cover two methods of distribution. First, there is the marketing of books through the mail, frequently by the book's publisher, occasionally by a bookseller. The larger facet of the field is mail order publishing, in which books are created specifically for the mail order market, especially in the form of the continuity series, a set of books with a common theme, offered to customers over a period of time. Either way, it is generally argued that, even more than book clubs, mail order sales reach people who otherwise do not buy books. In fact, the general manager of one of the major mail order publishers and sellers asserts that the best mailing lists are not necessarily those of magazine subscribers or book purchasers, but of previous mail order buyers of anything.

Publishing for mail order

Although magazine publishers may have been slow getting into the book club business, they were more attuned to publishing books to market to their own readers. The numbers involved are great and it is a difficult area of the business to break into in a small way.

Books created for the mail order market must typically carry a high unit price — some say a minimum of $12.95 these days. Books that are part of a continuity series, however, could be priced substantially lower, since it is anticipated that the people who respond will take at least several books in the set.

Continuity service

The cost of acquiring an order would follow that of the book club structure. Rarely, however, is there a substantial premium given, even with the series books, although some small giveaway (a pot holder or a poster) might be used in the series books. But the mail order publishers have a different set of uncertainties that must figure into their pricing. A book club gets a commitment from new members, so that the club knows the minimum it will sell and sets its prices accordingly, guaranteeing that should the member drop out after the minimum participation, the total acquisition costs will have been amortized. This is not so for the continuity publishers, since the only obligation of the respondent is to buy the first book in the series (and even this is offered on a no risk, trial basis). The continuity publishers, although not faced with the need to make advances and pay royalties, run the even greater risk of having to create the entire editorial package. Book clubs are merely marketers; the mail order business involves the greater up-front fixed costs of publishing, followed by the risk of marketing.

As a result, editorial ideas are usually extensively test marketed, a process that is unheard of in trade publishing. But mail order publishers can afford the luxury: when they publish a new series, they expect it to sell millions of copies over many years. But this is also why only the well financed can play. The biggest of the big is Time-Life Books, which has sold a staggering 200 million books since 1961 and produced revenues of $192 million in 1976 for Time Inc. (over 18% of its total). Meredith, American Heritage, and Reader's Digest are among the heavy weights that dominate the field. The all-time champion series is the Life Nature Library series, which has sold 40 million copies worldwide of its 26 volumes.

The life history of a continuity series begins, then, with a market test of the editorial concept. If the return should prove promising, editors will actually be assigned to start creating some real material, followed some months later by a larger, more ambitious mailing, often testing several different types of circulars and pricing approaches as well. Should this too prove responsive, final editorial plans are made and the major mailing is planned. In the case of Time-Life, the series on sewing started with a 12 million piece launch. Thus, by the time the first book is sent out, the combined editorial testing and major mailing costs could easily be in excess of $3 million. (Time-Life spends $250,000 *per volume* to create its series, before printing cost!) If the mailing yields an overall 2% return, then 240,000 orders are received, at $5.95 each, for $1.4 million in revenue (although offers usually permit recipients to return a book after inspecting it). Though printed on glossy paper with many four-color reproductions, the huge print runs result in low unit costs. At $2 per book, the first round of orders costs $480,000 to fulfill (again, postage and handling are added directly), plus $12.50 for acquisition and amortization of editorial expense for a total cost of $14.50. But as with the book clubs, the profits come with subsequent orders. With the purchase of a third book, the buyer has just about covered his cost of acquisition plus the cost of the books and beginning with the fourth book, under these assumptions, he begins contributing profusely to overhead and profit (see Table VIII-3).

From this point on, each order adds $3.95 to profit and overhead. Copies that are sent out but returned can be put back into inventory. Naturally, some people will drop out before purchasing four books, but others will buy 10, 12 or the entire set, with resulting margins that make the business so attractive.

Moreover, in these calculations, the initial acquisitions were presumed to have borne the entire burden of the editorial development expense, making future acquisitions look somewhat less expensive. Also, to the extent that the publisher uses in-house mailing lists cost per response is lower.

Continuity series books are also promoted in the mass media, often in the magazines of the publisher. Time-Life, for one, also has a network of 13 offices that attempt telephone sales, concentrating on calling to suburban Zip Code areas, but otherwise phoning cold turkey. Supermarket sales are a possibility with these series as well. Two-minute television and radio spots, usually in fringe hours, are also part of the media mix, with address as well as a toll-free phone number for responses. But direct mail still carries the overwhelming bulk of the promotion. Needless to say, mail order publishers are concerned by rapidly escalating postage rates, but there appears to be little chance of stopping their climb. But conventional channels have their cost pressures as well.

TABLE VIII-3:   Economics of Mail Order Continuity Publishing

	Per Customer
Editorial and acquisition cost (240,000 return on a 12 million piece mailing)	$12.50
Manufacturing cost, 4 volumes ($2,00@)	8.00
Total	$20.50
Revenue: $5.95 x 4 volumes	23.80
Contribution to profit and overhead	$ 3.30

Single volume, mail order publishing

It stands to reason that publishing a single volume for a primarily mail order market must rely on a different cost structure. For one thing, warns Meredith's former consumer book general manager, Jack Barlass, "It must be big enough and important enough to make all the economics work," meaning that it must justify a high enough price and appeal to a broad enough market. One-shot books can be combined in a catalogue or a mailing piece offering several books, thus increasing the potential dollar volume per order, or be included as stuffers in renewal notices for subscriptions. Having good mailing lists is essential. Thus, Meredith can afford to spend $10 per acquisition for its *Golden Treasury of Cooking*, plus $2 for printing and still have a healthy margin left at a price of $16.95.

Mailing order selling

Many trade houses have recognized that marketing their books through the mails and media directly to the consumer can have a multiple effect. Simon and Schuster is among the leaders in this area, with these sales alone bringing in $2 million in orders. Random House Enterprises, the direct mail arm of the publisher, is making a major effort in this direction. Herbert Nagourney, former president of The New York Times Book Co., looked at every new book with an eye toward its direct mail potential. For a standard trade title, the ability to find a mail order audience has at least five potential benefits:

• It gives the book a longer life. Sales are not dependent on the bookseller having the book in stock, and do not end when the retailer decides to replace the title with a newer one. Although bestsellers do not fit this scheme, typical backlist titles on gardening, cooking, management, home repairs, and self-improvement are all good candidates.

• Mail order advertising exposure can aid bookstore sales. A large space coupon advertisement may not pay for itself directly in responses, but the advertisement is also serving the purpose of pushing the title in the stores. Meredith attributes its strong showing of the *Family Medical Guide* in bookstores to its extensive mail order promotion. And in direct orders, the publisher keeps the 40% discount given the retailer, a cumulative sum that alone may carry the cost of the advertisement.

• The mail order ad exposure may also create the added interest to enable the book to get a larger guarantee from a paperback house or be picked as a book club selection.

• Up to 70% of mail orders come accompanied by cash, which, given the cost of money, is a distinct advantage.

• By broadening the market for a book through the mail, the book may be priced lower. A book planned just for the retail market, necessitating a small print run, would have to cost more than one with an expanded audience through mail orders.

Specialized publishers

Publishers of highly specialized professional books rely greatly on mail order selling. Because their titles are directed toward a readily identifiable audience, they can acquire mailing lists that return much higher percentages of orders than the general consumer mail order publishers. One example would be many R.R. Bowker titles, such as the *Directory of American Scholars* (at $39.50 per volume), which have very limited, but concentrated markets. Hastings House sends mailings for its Communication Arts books to the faculties of university communications schools resulting in orders for personal libraries as well as possible textbook use. Publishers such as Richard D. Irwin solicit orders for many of their business books through advertisements in *The Wall Street Journal*. Given the higher price of these books and the above average response, they can be quite profitable despite sales of 2000 or fewer through these channels.

For many business and professional book publishers, selling by direct mail and coupons is essential to their survival, since bookstores will not carry enough of their titles or do not reach the specialized audiences for these titles. Over a period of years, the cumulative sales of even specialized titles can approach bestseller proportions, even though such books never appear on any bestseller list. Prentice-Hall, a master of direct mail for the single title, has sold over 100,000 copies of a book called *The Management of Time* since its introduction more than a dozen years ago.

Finally, mail order is also vital for the scholarly and university press, with similarly limited access to bookstore outlets. A typical book from these publishers may sell 50% of its units to libraries, 35%-40% to individual mail order buyers, and only 10%-15% to bookstore buyers.

Retail stores are not abdicating the mails to publishers. They too use advertising in the media and catalogues to expand their market. Brentano's has cut down on its regular advertising, but does promote special titles, accompanied by coupons, in newspapers. One advertisement featured "Jane's" books, along with a selection of paperbacks for $.69 to $.99 each (although a $.50 per book postage charge leaned heavily on the latter). Scribner's Bookstore went with *The Wall Street Journal* for a full page pre-Christmas advertisement combining bestsellers with expensive "coffee table" gift ideas. R.R. Bowker offers a standard Christmas book catalogue to retailers, with their own name imprinted thereon, to send to customers.

STRENGTHS AND WEAKNESSES OF MAIL ORDER DISTRIBUTION

As a method for publishing and distributing books, direct mail can be highly profitable, while benefitting the consumer. It is good for publishing generally because it is widely thought of as expanding the market for bookbuyers. In particular, the continuity series of Time-Life, Newsweek, and American Heritage are aimed at families with children. The books are sold as being useful: good for reference, educational, and entertaining. It is not likely that a fraction of these books would have been sold if left to trade channels. The one-shot, how-to and reference books are likewise brought to the attention of a much broader audience than would otherwise be possible. The volume production of these books, compared to print runs of trade books, makes them more affordable — and profitable.

To the extent that trade publishers can increase their sales through direct selling, they too can take advantage of the economies. Even small booksellers who cannot afford to buy large advertisements can get fallout from space and direct mail promotions of the publishers. Witness the sales of Meredith's medical guide, or the sales of the Newsweek and Time-Life series books in the bookstores (at a few dollars more than their mail order price, to keep everyone happy). Though Time-Life estimates that less than 10% of its books are sold through bookstores, that is still 10% of a very large total.

Probably the biggest deterrent to the greater use of this form of distribution is the major entry costs. Although publishing is known as a field with easy entry, the heavy reliance on the mails, the need for acquisition of mailing lists, test marketing lists and concepts, and the development of editorial material that has the potential for a broad appeal make this form of publishing prohibitive to the small business or the faint of heart. Recent times have also shown mail order selling quite susceptible to swings in the economy, with mail order publishers suffering through a bad 1975. Each time a new book arrives, the customer has to decide whether to keep it. And, unlike the impulse buying that is frequently prevalent in bookstore sales (see Chapter IV), direct mail purchasers must make very conscious buying decisions in the realities of their own home. In a time of recession and inflation, that decision is more likely to be "no."

Everyone who sells by direct mail is feeling the pressure of rapidly rising postage costs, especially third class. The bulk mail rate nearly doubled between 1970 and 1976 from $40 per 1000 pieces to $79 per 1000. This increases the cost of a million piece mailing by $39,000 or about $1.95 per acquisition. The continuity publishers also get stuck when manufacturing costs escalate rapidly: although they can change the announced cost per book in new mailings, old customers must be permitted to continue the series at the old price.

Direct mail selling of books is still in its relative infancy and the full ingenuity of publishers and marketers has not yet come to full fruition. For example, there is a largely untapped field of syndicated packages, such as those put together by Doubleday's J.G. Ferguson division, which creates direct mail books and mailing pieces to be sold by Amoco (Standard Oil of Indiana), through its credit card operation. And whereas most continuity series have aimed at the low end of the market, one gambit was a luxury limited edition of the 49 Pulitzer Prize winning works of fiction, bound in leather and ornamented in 22 karat gold. Offered by the Franklin Mint, the series (limit of one to a person, please) costs only $1372 over four years. They announced the series as being "fully subscribed."

CONCENTRATION OF AND LEADING COMPANIES IN MAIL ORDER AND BOOK CLUBS

Although there are niches for the little fellow, the book club and mail order businesses are both dominated by giant companies. In book clubs, two companies, Doubleday and Book-of-the-Month, have more than half the estimated total of $343.1 million in annual sales. In mail order the dominance is even more striking: one company, Time Inc., accounts for 55% of the $348.9 million total. Table VIII-4 gives estimates of revenues and profits for the five largest companies in mail order and book club operations.

TABLE VIII-4:   Five Largest Mail Order and Book Club Companies, 1976 (in millions)

Company	Revenues
Time Inc.*	$192
Doubleday	105
Reader's Digest	100
Grolier	77
Book-of-the Month Club	65

*Time Inc. acquired Book-of-the-Month Club in 1977.

SOURCE: Knowledge Industry Publications, Inc.

Unlike other segments of the book business, however, mail order and book clubs may have reached the natural limits of market concentration. Certainly Doubleday and BOMC had experienced only modest revenue growth in recent years, whereas Time-Life Books' growth has been propelled mostly by overseas expansion. In contrast, some of the fastest growth has come from the specialized clubs run by Macmillan or McGraw-Hill. There are certainly economies of scale in both book clubs and mail order publishing that favor the bigger companies – but the sometimes lackluster profit margins at a company like Time-Life Books suggest that the inertia and exorbitant overhead of large companies can be a negative factor as well.

SUMMARY

Book clubs have become an established element in the distribution of books published by trade houses, whereas mail order publishing and sales are a growing segment of the industry. To the extent they broaden the market for books and make them more available, the argument is very persuasive that they create more book sales, rather than merely shifting the source of sales from the bookstores. Nonetheless, direct mail marketing can never be more than a supplementary mode of distribution. It is expensive and risky; the past several years have shown that even book clubs with built-in mailing lists from magazines will not have an easy path to success. The special interest book clubs tap a vein of book buyers who might otherwise be lost, but the numbers for each club are rather small, for example 80,000 in one, 165,000 in another. The ability of Book-of-the-Month's Quality Paperback Book Service to find a niche will depend largely on its success in shaking out the rights to trade paperback editions of bestsellers.

The disadvantages of mail order are the lack of a "hands-on" feel, the elimination of the impulse sale, and the relatively few number of books that can be economically sold via mail response and ad coupon clipping. For the publishing industry, sales through the mail is a promising source for additional revenue and a mode of distribution that will grow as the total industry expands. But it is not an answer to the difficulties of distribution through retail outlets.

IX

Retail Bookselling

Although the *American Book Trade Directory* identifies 16,217 outlets for books in the United States as of early 1977, only 12,926 can be considered to be bookstores. As seen in Table IX-1, the others include antiquarian stores that deal in old books, gift shops or sundry other shops that carry books distinctly as a sideline. Although all book outlets have increased 51% since 1971, the increase in bookstores is somewhat greater, at 60%. General bookstores make up nearly one-third of the total, and have shown

TABLE IX-1: Bookstores in the United States, 1971 and 1977

	1971	% of total	1977	% of total	% change 1971-1977
Bookstores					
General	2468	30.5	4281	33.1	73.5
Religious	1638	20.2	2752	21.3	68.0
College	2265	28.0	2607	20.2	15.1
Juvenile & Specialized	NA	—	1118	8.6	—
Department Stores	901	11.1	1089	8.4	20.9
Professional	171	2.1	203	1.6	18.7
Foreign language	65	0.8	76	0.6	16.9
Paperback	591	7.3	800	6.2	35.4
Total	8099	100.0	12,926	100.0	59.6
Miscellaneous stores Drug, gift, office supply, antiquarian, stationers, news-dealers, etc.	2643		3291		40.5
Total	10,742		16,217		51.0

NA - not available
SOURCE: R.R. Bowker Co., *American Book Trade Directory,* 1971-72 and 1977·

the most dramatic increase. The U.S. Commerce Department's 1972 Census of Retail Trade provides outdated figures, enumerating 7830 retail bookstores, plus another 1117 that sell books as a sideline or by direct mail.

ECONOMICS OF STORES

Most serious booksellers belong to the American Booksellers Association, a trade group formed in 1900. Dues to the ABA are assessed on each bookstore or chain based on its gross receipts. As of June 30, 1973, the ABA counted 3324 stores, including 458 branch stores, 506 department stores and branches, and 102 foreign outlets. As determined by their dues category, Table IX-2 shows that 55% of these stores had under $100,000 in receipts, whereas 12% had sales exceeding $5 million.

TABLE IX-2: Bookstores by Total Receipts

Receipts	ABA Members	
	Percent	Cumulative Percent
Under $50,000	27.6	27.6
$50,000 to 99,999	27.6	55.2
$100,000 to 299,999	10.1	65.3
$300,000 to 999,999	9.2	74.5
$1 million to 2,999,999	7.2	81.7
$3 million to 4,999,999	5.9	87.6
$5 million or more	12.4	100.0

Number of stores: ABA-3324; Department of Commerce-2960.

SOURCE: American Booksellers Association, June 30, 1973.

Bookselling remains a unique type of business, dominated by small "Mom and Pop" operations. Table IX-3 compares bookstores with several other retail trades. The booksellers have low per store volume and only 64% have any payroll.

The most recent U.S. Department of Commerce data indicate that over 94% of all bookstores are run by single establishment

TABLE IX-3: Bookstores and Other Retail Trades

	Bookstores	Drugstores	Auto and Home Supply Stores
Number	7830	51,542	37,510
Sales			
(million $)	$907.0	15,599.0	3,542.8
Average sales/store	$115,840	302,645	94,451
Sole proprietor (%)	47.4	27.9	38.1
1000 population/store	26.6	4.0	5.6

SOURCE: U.S. Department of Commerce, 1972 *Census of Retail Trade.*

firms. But the 4.2% of the retail firms which have more than a single outlet run nearly 19% of the 7830 total bookselling establishments (Table IX-4). Similarly, the 3.7% of the firms which reported sales in 1972 of more than $500,000 accounted for over 53% of total bookstore revenue. Nonetheless, compared to retail trade in general,

TABLE IX-4: Single and Multiunit Retail Book Establishments, 1972

	Number of Establishments	Number of Firms Owning	· % of Total Firms
Single units, Total	6,359	6,359	95.8
operated by 1-unit firms	6,250	6,250	94.1
operated as part of multi-establishment firm	109	109	1.6
Multiunits, Total	1,471	281	4.2
2 units	292	146	2.2
3 units	177	59	0.8
4 to 5 units	163	37	0.6
6 to 10 units	165	24	0.4
11 to 25 units	128	7	0.1
26 to 50 units	134	4	*
51 to 100 units	202	3	*
101 or more units	210	1	*
Total	7,830	6,640	100.0

* less than 0.1%

SOURCE: U.S Bureau of the Census, *Census of Retail Trade,* 1972 (SIC 5942)

bookselling still exhibits far greater influence on the part of smaller firms. Whereas in bookselling, firms under $500,000 did 46.8% of the volume (Table IX-5), in retail trade as a whole, firms of this size did just 30% of the volume.

TABLE IX-5: Retail Book Establishments by Revenues, 1972
(SIC 5942)

Size of Firms (000)	Number of Firms	Sales (000)	% of Total Sales
$100,000 or more	—	—	—
50,000 to 99,999	—	—	—
25,000 to 49,999	2	*	} 11.0
20,000 to 24,999	1	*	
15,000 to 19,999	—	—	—
10,000 to 14,999	3	$39,395	4.3
5,000 to 9,999	9	59,486	6.6
1,000 to 4,999	91	182,047	20.1
500 to 999	141	101,541	11.2
Under 500	6393	424,595	46.8
Total retail book establishments	6640	$907,027	100.0

*Deleted to protect confidential information.

SOURCE: U.S. Bureau of Census, *Census of Retail Trade,* 1972.

The operations of bookstores are similar to those of other retail businesses handling durable goods of small unit value. But bookseller experience, as well as surveys such as that in Chapter IV, indicate that the bookstore has the particularly crucial function of providing an opportunity for browsing that contributes to the spontaneous nature of much book buying.

Certain complexities of bookselling make it a business with more extreme characteristics than possibly any other retail business. The chief one is the enormous body of product from which a retailer must select inventory. There were over 478,000 books of all kinds in print in 1977, with upwards of 27,000 new titles and 8000 new editions being added each year, while only 15,000 titles go out of print. Booksellers must familiarize themselves with many of these, as well as obtain and maintain an inventory. For some, the task is more defined: a medical bookseller has a boundary on the titles that are available for consideration; a paperback store at least can disregard most hardcover titles. But this is still scant help. There are, for example, over 26,000 medical books in print, 123,000 paperbound titles. The largest general bookstores carry 30,000 titles at most, with 5000 to 18,000 being far more prevalent. In contrast, an average supermarket stocks 6500 items — and with far fewer new ones competing for shelf space each year.

Yet the book buying public expects from the bookseller a service that other retailers are rarely called upon to make, that is, the special ordering of books that are not — cannot be — in stock. Just to have the capability to look up a book requires an impressive and expensive array of materials. The four volume *Books in Print* costs $86.50 (issued annually), its midyear supplement costs $42.50. The booksellers who take special orders, an overwhelming majority, then incur expenses in filling out forms, tracing the proper book, and handling the order.

A small bookstore can provide a modest living for its owner, as well as a decent return on his investment. As in most businesses, there are certain economies with increased size that make larger stores relatively more profitable. Table IX-6 presents KIPI estimates of typical income and expense components for two sizes of stores that make up the bulk of the individually owned and operated bookstores. Rents represent locations in suburban malls or many downtown areas. Since inventory turnover should be at least three times annually, or, with many paperbacks, more like five times, the smaller store, with a decent four times turnover, would have an inventory, at cost, of about $16,000. Thus, net income (before taxes) would represent a return on investment in inventory of 18%, whereas similar figures for the larger operation could be closer to 40% (again, this is before taxes). Chain stores would have a decidedly higher gross margin, but they would have to allocate a percentage toward corporate services and overhead.

Of course, many bookstores do not make any money, with as many as a third ending the year with a loss. Stores have traditionally used a rule of thumb of sales per square feet as a standard for measuring business, with $80 per foot a current

figure. The chain operations expect more, and some very successful stores generate over twice this amount. But there are still many
small bookstores that cram thousands of books, spine out, into
450 square feet, so that even at $110 a foot in sales, it is a struggle
to support more than a single owner/operator. Any bookstore
under 1000 square feet is destined to remain a marginal operation.

TABLE IX-6: Percentage Income Statement for Individually Owned
Bookstore

	Revenue	
	$100,000	$300,000
Total	100.0%	100.0%
Cost of sales	63.0	62.0
Gross profit	37.0%	38.0%
Operating expenses		
Rent	6.0%	5.0%
Utilities	1.2	1.0
Insurance and accounting	1.2	0.6
Salaries[1]	20.0	18.0
Telephone	0.5	0.3
Freight/postage	1.8	1.8
Taxes, licenses	0.2	0.1
Repair and maintenance	0.4	0.2
Office supplies	0.3	0.2
Dues and subscriptions	0.2	0.1
Miscellaneoius	0.2	0.2
Advertising	1.0	1.0
Depreciation and interest	1.0	1.0
	34.0%	29.5%
Income before		
State and federal taxes	3.0	8.5
Inventory turnover	4x	4x

[1] Includes owner's salary.

THE CHAIN STORES: HEROES OR VILLAINS?

Perhaps the most vociferous debate among booksellers today involves the invasion of book land by major mass marketers who, their critics charge, peddle books like soap or groceries. Among the relative newcomers to the club are Walden Book Co., a subsidiary of the giant ($1.4 billion in sales in 1976) Carter Hawley Hale Stores, and B. Dalton Booksellers, owned by Dayton Hudson Corp. ($1.9 billion in 1976 sales). These two chains alone currently own about 700 stores between them and on many first printings will account for over 10% of a trade publisher's orders. Chains themselves are not actually new: Doubleday has 32 stores around the country; Brentano's, and Kroch's & Brentano's, have been regional chains. But Walden and Dalton are the first to tackle bookselling on a national scale. Given the previous lack of concentration in bookselling, the big concern is the impact that two chains can have when they control a fifth of the general bookstores in the United States.

The chains' benefits

Bringing in their ability for mass buying at top discounts (see analysis of discounts), their computerized inventory, and their clout with publishers, the chains do not seem to fit into the genteel bookseller's world. However, there is much to support the hypothesis that the chains are a good thing for publishing. Among the reasons are the following:

- They are remedying one of the most frequently heard complaints in the book business: lack of retail outlets. Both firms have concentrated their growth outside of the heavily blanketed Northeast, favoring suburban shopping malls in the Midwest, Southwest, and South.

- They are better stocked with many titles because of the inventory record sent to corporate headquarters weekly, with ensuing computer printouts of needs. (But both give local stores leeway in ordering hot items from local jobbers.)

• They advertise. Their cooperative advertising money from publishers becomes sizable thanks to their overall volume, and their concentration of several stores in a single trading area makes advertising more economically feasible (although Dalton claims to spend less than the average retailer's percent of sales overall).

• They know that to make big profits they must expand the market for books beyond the customary serious book buyer. Thus, they must rely on mass merchandising techniques to get people who have never gone into a bookstore to come in and browse, and then have enough of a selection to get a sale.

• To the extent that they open up new outlets and bring in new customers, the chains are increasing overall book sales, as well as adding a degree of efficiency, so that publishers can sell 530 stores with a visit to two customers. The two big chains in 1977 sold over 90 million books worth over $280 million at retail. It can be argued reasonably that many of those sales would not have been made without the stores opened by Walden and Dalton.

A few publishers and more traditional booksellers take a less positive − or downright antagonistic − view of the chain stores, arguing that:

• Although chains may make the industry more efficient, there is the fear that the standardization of book buying on works of only mass appeal will doom less popular books of merit, or the work of the new novelist.

• To meet corporate profitability quotas, the chain stores must rely on a fast turnover, meaning a stock of only bestsellers and other fast movers.

• The prime mall locations and mass purchasing discounts give the chains an unfair advantage over independent booksellers and will drive them out of the marketplace.

Events do not seem to be supporting the naysayers. True, Walden has been able to lean on publishers for better discounts.

But it has also alerted publishers to the need for certain books, as a result of feedback from its vast network of stores. When the demand for books on backgammon and needlepoint became obvious, Walden took the ideas to several major publishers who commissioned books on these subjects. The guaranteed sale through Walden alone could make publication profitable. By their extensive coverage, the chains can engage in an informal sort of market research — an area in which most publishers do little if any work. Moreover, as ABA Executive Director G. Royce Smith is wont to point out, "If there are readers for books, they will get published and there will be bookstores to sell them. . . . If the chains choose not to buy a title which would not have been made prior to the existence of the chains, it is false to argue that the chains prevented publication of the book."

In addition, it is really a spurious argument that the chains carry only a few books. True, the average Waldenbook store does not have much more than 8000 titles, but management is sensitive to this and is working to expand the number. "We can't make a go of it by catering only to readers who like bestsellers," explains Walden's president Russell Hoyt. "To make it in the book business, you have to concentrate on a much broader market segment." The B. Dalton stores, in fact, are as complete as any of the major stores — highlighting the fact that even among chains there are distinctive differences in marketing philosophies. The average Dalton store carries nearly 30,000 titles (20,000 for an average Brentano's). Unlike Waldenbooks, Dalton will handle special orders for customers. "We don't make any money at it, but it's necessary for customer service," admits a Dalton executive. Although the same official admits that for many major chains (other than his own) the lack of interest in buying the book of a first-time novelist is "justifiable," he adds that Dalton does buy such books in small quantities, to promote the image of a full-service bookstore. "If we back off hardcover fiction, it's because it's not selling to the public. We're letting the public lead us, we don't lead the public."

The chain stores do look for a turnover in the upper end of the three to five times average book turnover range, but then, what bookseller shouldn't? They do this with remainder tables, fine-tuning the paperback/hardcover mix, and certainly by attractive merchandising. "The key to growth is reaching the casual book buyer," notes one observer, and that is done through good location as much as any other technique. Both Walden and Dalton look for sites with strong national and local chains in the mall and the potential for up to $125 in sales per square foot per year (and slightly more in downtown stores).

Table IX-7 estimates the sales and market share of the five leading chains in 1977. Even with the considerable growth of the chains in the past five years, their share of the total market is not dominating, indicating that retail bookselling is considerably less concentrated than various segments of the publishing industry.

TABLE IX-7: Size and Revenues of the Leading Bookstore Chains, 1977

	No. of Stores	Revenues (millions)	Share of Market, Total Bookstore Sales
1. Carter Hawley Hale/ Walden Book Co.	400	$146	9.3%
2. Dayton-Hudson/ B. Dalton	300	135	9.0
3. Kroch's & Brentano's	20	25	1.7
4. Doubleday	32	17	1.1
5. Macmillan/ Brentano's	27	15	1.0
Five largest chains	779	$332	22.1%

SOURCE: Knowledge Industry Publications estimate.

Role of independents

The argument that chain stores can drive out independents through better location and lower buying costs is an old one and precedes the entry of mass merchandisers into bookstores. Supermarkets were to be the demise of the local grocery store, and the discount department stores of the local specialty shops. Yet local shops — with good management — have other tools at their disposal: flexibility in making decisions, the ability to move quickly, individuality, extra services. One cannot go into Sessler's in Philadelphia, for example, and envision this full-line store being threatened by a Waldenbooks: an independent bookseller can create an ambience, a personal touch, and more specialized services than a homogenized chain operation. At the same time, independent booksellers should take notice that there are opportunities for expansion. By taking advantage of local goodwill and knowledge of the territory, the expanding independent business can gain several of the discount, advertising, and overhead economies of the national chains.

Nor must a store be part of a large chain to be very profitable. In its six years of operation, a North Dallas, Texas entrepreneur has built his family owned and run bookstore into almost a $1 million operation. Having expanded twice in that period, the store has 5200 square feet, meaning that its sales are around $190 per foot. The store, Preston Books, has grown at a compounded rate of about 100% per year. The success results from the owner's recognition of opportunity and a sound business approach to the operation. "Dallas didn't have a 'full-service' book store and we believed that if we provided one we would sell a lot of books," explains owner Henry Taylor. Ironically, Taylor attributes his strong growth largely to his lack of literary inclination and his corresponding flair for merchandising.

The chain stores are as much a threat to the bookselling industry now as book clubs were perceived to have been 40 years ago. They are viewed with most alarm by those who have a snooty or nonbusiness view of bookdom — the very attitudes that for too long have kept bookselling confined, old-fashioned, and inaccessible to the majority of potential customers.

DISCOUNTS AND PRICING

As explained in Chapter V, bookstores buy from either the publishers directly or from jobbers and wholesalers, at discounts varying from 20% to 46%, but averaging close to 40% for most books. Large and multistore operations do have the advantage of 43% to 46% discounts by bulk ordering for their stores, with some of the extra margin covering corporate overhead, some ending up on the bottom line — the difference between the marginal small stores and the attractiveness of the chains. But according to provisions of the Robinson-Patman Act, manufacturers can only offer varying discounts when they reflect a real cost savings to the manufacturer.

In mid-1974, Doubleday announced that it would no longer give bulk discounts to chain stores if it involved drop-shipping parts of the order to each individual store. The small stores quietly smiled, but Dalton and Walden were vocally upset. Neither Dalton nor Walden had major central warehousing facilities and did not want to be in the distribution business. Dalton boycotted Doubleday altogether, whereas Waldenbooks gradually cut its purchases from Doubleday. A year later, faced with a loss in sales that easily exceeded $1 million, Doubleday yielded. It granted the higher discounts, with the chains for their part agreeing to pay the shipping costs to each store (as opposed to the much lower bulk cost of taking delivery at a central point). Since the four or five percentage points of gross margin was a far larger sum than the drop-ship costs, the clout of the chains was clearly impressed on even the biggest publishers. (At the same time, Doubleday revised its discount schedule to allow a higher discount for stores ordering assorted titles, thus easing the position of the independent booksellers as well.)

Bookselling has seemingly always been on a list price basis. Unlike other industries, especially those without known brands or easily recognized standard products, books are sold at a discount from an established list price set by manufacturers. Because of the relatively slim gross margins, there has been precious little retail discounting of book prices, other than the book clubs (but even in their case, added postage and handling charges dilute such reductions in price). Fair trade laws in most states had also helped maintain the publishers' price list, but even that did not stop scattered discounting by stores such as Korvettes, which at one point had been enjoined in New York from selling a $4.00 list book for $2.79. But the ineffectiveness of fair trade resulted in its erosion in state after state and it has been repealed, one outcome of the consumerist movement. (Recently, Barnes & Noble in New York has advertised all 20 books on the *New York Times* bestseller list at about 40% off list, or approximately its cost − an obvious promotional and traffic-building tactic.)

Some publishers have toyed with the idea of abandoning list prices in favor of selling at a net cost. Retailers would then add whatever markup they wish and put their own sticker on the book. This is attractive to publishers because royalties are tied to list price and any time they increase this, part of the rise automatically goes to the author. But the booksellers are afraid of net pricing, for good reasons. For one thing, that means that each book will have to be individually priced, a costly process involving checking the invoice price for each book, figuring out the margin, performing the calculation, and printing up and attaching price stickers — which would have to be removed from returns. Moreover, writes the ABA's Royce Smith, net pricing would result in price wars — battles for which the small bookseller is least equipped to win. To date, there has not been a major push for the abandonment of list pricing by any segment of the industry. However, if the chains begin to lobby for a change, it may not be too difficult to convince the publishers.

TRENDS IN RETAIL BOOK SELLING

Besides the sudden interest of major retailing chains in book retailing, several other developments are promising signs of greater vigor in this end of the industry. Already discussed in Chapter VII is the effort of some distributors to expand book sales in national retail operations such as Penney's and Sears, as well as the supermarket outlets, and Doubleday's experiments in signing up book club members through the food stores.

Specialty stores

Bookstores that specialize in a particular type of book are not new, but in a time of rapidly diversifying interests, the specialist is often the answer to the mushrooming number of book titles. Bowker's *American Book Trade Directory* for 1977-78 lists 124 special stores, as well as 93 educational, 76 foreign language, 94 juvenile, 58 law, 97 medical, and 48 science-technology stores. A new bookstore in Philadelphia, Garlands of Roses, deals exclusively in books on yoga and transcendental meditation, whereas the more well-known How-To Bookstore is replete with just that genre. Seattle has a store devoted solely to the occult. New York's Liberia Hispanica stocks 45,000 Spanish language books for the city's large Spanish-speaking community. California has at least eight stores selling only children's books.

Specialty stores still take a back seat to direct mail in getting books to target audiences. But one way the small bookseller can respond to the bigness of the competing chains and the overwhelming tide of new books is through specialization. The concept of a single general bookstore servicing all needs is not as viable as it once was. One avenue to success in bookselling may well be in zeroing in on concentrated markets. Barnes & Noble, the long time textbook specialist, is encouraged enough to not only remodel and expand its lower Fifth Avenue New York store but has actually embarked on establishing a small chain of special interest stores, opening in the same suburban malls that the general store chains have chosen.

Paperback stores

In 1961, only 2.6% of bookstores were classified as primarily dealing in paperbacks. By 1977, this percentage had more than doubled to 6.2%, with 800 booksellers having stock consisting of at least 80% paperbacks. There is even a franchise chain, Paperback Booksmith, with over 50 stores on the East Coast.

Paperback store economics have been aided by three phenomena. First, the rapid increase in the price of paperbacks has made their sale more profitable, whereas the even quicker climb of hardcover prices has made the mass market paperbacks relatively as attractive as ever. Second, there have been more original paperbacks, not just the westerns and romances, but also the "instant" Bantam and Dell books on major topics. Bantam took a February, 1975, *Esquire* article on the economy by futurist Alvin Toffler, asked the author to expand it threefold, and had a book, *The Eco-Spasm Report*, in bookstores by May, 1975. Coincidently with such activity, the major book review media are giving increasing attention to paperbacks in general and originals in particular. Third, the highly illustrated and attractive trade paperbacks have added a new dimension of prestige, depth, and quality to all bookstores, but paperback bookstores now have more to stock and can appeal to an audience that may shun the mass market books, but will accept the trade paperbacks. These books, priced at $3.95 or more, further benefit the economics of a paperback operation.

Franchise bookstores

One of the quickest ways of expanding a name is through a good franchise system. Paperback Booksmith began with three stores in 1961, and now has over 50. The Little Professor Book Centers, affiliated with Maple Press, has 75 stores in 28 states. For about $55,000, Little Professor provides a package that includes everything from site selection to fixtures, an inventory of hard and softbound books worth $38,000 at list price, and even a grand opening advertising promotion. Both Little Professor and Book-smith have their own distributing companies, so that their stores can (though they don't have to) do most purchasing centrally. Little Professor also provides weekly fiche inventory information, similar to Ingram's system, as well as computer stock cards to aid in reordering. Both chains have promoted themselves actively, with Little Professor running franchise ads in the *Wall Street Journal.* These stores are bright and open and designed to produce sales of at least $100,000. Although there are many arguments against going into a franchise (at least one is the 4.25% of gross off the top to Little Professor as a yearly fee), the franchises do provide for entry into the business by many more people and, through their standardized procedures and training programs optimize the chances that the stores will be efficiently managed and well stocked.

College stores

College stores have traditionally been the source for students to get their required course textbooks, plus university mugs, sweat shirts, records, and toiletries. They are run by managers who are not particularly pressured into making money and want no headaches with book ordering, returns, and the like. Nonetheless, many do a considerable trade and mass market book business, exemplified best by the Harvard Coop, with its three floors of hardcover, paperbacks, and textbooks. College stores did a gross volume in 1976-77 conservatively estimated at over $1.2 billion, 60% of which came from books. Of the $720 million from books, $364 million in sales were from trade, professional, mass market, and other nontextbook categories. Much of this total comes from course related purchases of these types of books. The fact remains that college bookstores have a built-in market for general books, not only among the students but among the faculty and administrators as well. In many smaller towns, the college bookstore may be the only full bookstore around. For example, at small (2400 enrollment) Seattle Pacific College, the bookstore shares a building with a national bank. In its first year in the new location, profits of the store were up 35%, with 10% of total store sales attributable to noncampus customers.

Bookseller displays at conventions of college bookstore managers have not gone over with outstanding results. But increased promotion in this area appears advisable. Mass market and trade books, with the 35%-40% discounts, are far more profitable than textbooks with 20% discounts. More crucial, textbook sales invariably are concentrated in two or three brief selling seasons. Expanded general book sections can help keep up sales throughout the year. The National Association of College Stores has recognized the growing role of general books by starting its own wholesaler distributorship, carrying steadily demanded trade and mass market paperbacks.

New merchandising techniques

Bookstores usually display their books by subject matter, except for mass market paperback sections, which often have separate sections arranged by publisher. In fact, one of the holdovers from the early days of paperbacks is their segregation from hardcover books. At Brentano's on Fifth Avenue in New York City, for example, paperbacks still have second-class status in the basement. But a change is nigh: Brentano's is now experimenting with a single system, integrating all books by category. The expansion of the trade paperbacks may have heightened this trend: there was no move to start a third section for these books, and if cloth and paper were to commingle, why not go all the way? In its first applications, the technique has increased paperback sales dramatically. Brentano's is less certain of its effect on hardcover sales.

Another approach is the adaptation of a classification system for each book that may result in its being displayed in more than one category. Why not put *Essays of E.B. White* with literature, as well as with best sellers? The biography of a sports star should be under biography *and* sports. This increases its potential audience, since many titles cut across several fields. There are inventory problems — and it may mean ordering more copies of each title — but the practice makes much intuitive sense, and at least one bookseller who is organized this way has found it worthwhile.

Remainders

Remainders and low cost hardcover reprints have become for many the elixir in an otherwise dull business climate. Remainders are copies of a book that publishers (and booksellers) have given up trying to sell at the original price. Because they are sold at distress sale prices (perhaps 10% of their original list), they end up on special sale tables of retailers at half or less of their original price — which, thanks to printed-on list prices, can always be checked by an ever skeptical consuming public. The chain stores were the first retailers to see the beauty of the remainder business on a large scale. And, rather than hurting other sales, remainders became just the draw that the stores needed to increase store traffic. Remainders are usually sold from large tables in the front of the store, often grouped by price.

These books (and their reprint cousins) offer booksellers the sorely needed low-cost merchandise that they cannot get from the publishers directly, since, unlike other retail businesses that take slow moving goods for markdowns, booksellers have the return privilege, making markdowns unnecessary. Enter the remainder wholesalers, led by Outlet Books, Harlem Book Co., and A&W Promotional Book Corp. They buy the publishers' overstocks by bidding on them by lots. Retailers then buy them either in package deals, with the wholesaler putting the package together, limited by the amount of money the retailer wants to spend, or by picking specific titles from a catalogue or showroom. Consistent with industry practices, the wholesaler determines the "sale" price for each book (what the retailer should sell it for), then offers the usual 40% off this price, with returns allowed. Returns average about 20%. However, Walden has started its own remainder distribution operation and has been offering a 50% discount with no returns, particularly popular for distant customers who must pay 5% or 6% in freight charges. About half of Walden's customers have elected this option.

Remainders are profitable to the bookseller for three reasons. First, they build traffic for the store. Since much of book buying is on impulse, getting people into the shop is half the battle. Second, they have the same margin as other trade books, but they should have a faster turnover. And since they are best sold in mass displays stacked on tables, more books can be accommodated in a smaller space than otherwise. Psychologically, customers feel better about spending $9.98 for a large, four-color, illustrated $25 list price book on the history of film than on a thin bestseller. Finally, they help the image of the store, since they are examples of providing good value. (See Chapter XII for more on remaindering and reprints).

THE SPECIAL ORDER PROBLEM

For the full-service bookstore, special orders are a way of life. With 478,000 titles in print to choose from and 10,000 to 30,000 titles in stock at any moment, it is inevitable that on any given day, more than one customer will request a book that the seller does not usually carry. Often, that is the end of it. But the customer may ask if the bookseller could get it. Although some booksellers eschew such special orders, others find it worthwhile, not because it is profitable in itself, but for the goodwill. Moreover, it gets book buyers into the store at least twice, once to place the order, again to pick it up. Given the impulse nature of book purchases, others may be bought. Sessler's in Philadelphia averages 60 special orders a week, the Yale Co-Op, as many as 200.

Under favorable circumstances, special orders can be bunched with regular orders to publishers, who give the regular discount, but with a wait of four to six weeks. If it is not too obscure a title, a jobber might have it and it could be included in that order. But most of the time, the jobber does not have the title and the customer does not want to wait so long. Hence, the booksellers and publishers got together with a Single Copy Order Plan (SCOP). Thus, instead of putting through the request as a regular order to the publisher, at a "short" (20%) discount, the bookseller fills out a special SCOP order form and includes a check for the book ordered, at list less the publishers' prescribed SCOP discount (70% of a survey of 208 publishers offered 40%, only 8% gave less than 30% off). The publisher then sends the book to the store, saving invoicing and billing. A special order using SCOP sometimes takes only days to receive, but, as one bookseller complains, at other times it has taken two months. SCOP must be considered mainly as a goodwill gesture to the booksellers, just as special orders are a favor to customers – no one makes much money on them. The bookseller, in fact, would have no alternative except to refuse all special orders if the publishers would only give a 20% discount, since there is no substitutability for many specific books.

The SCOP plan has been one bright example of publisher/ bookseller cooperation in solving a widespread industry problem. Unfortunately, it is less effective than ever today. Booksellers get the price of the book from *Books in Print*, an R.R. Bowker publication that lists all books. However, ballooning publishing costs have resulted in numerous price changes, so that special order departments find that many of the SCOPs are coming back for checks reflecting the revised price – and thus short-circuiting the whole procedure. (Bowker has responded in part by publishing a midyear supplement to *Books in Print*, showing price changes as well as newly out-of-print books.) Moreover, only 20% of publishers participate in SCOP (albeit the major ones).

An attempt to bypass the changing price problem (as well as handle situations where several books are being ordered from a publisher and some are not available, or the wrong discount is calculated, or insufficient postage included) has been dubbed BCO – Blank Check Orders. As it implies, the bookseller sends a SCOP order, but attaches a blank check, which the publisher fills in based on what is shipped and the attendant postage. This solution was devised by an enterprising California bookseller.

Such plans, although helpful, still accentuate the same problem that booksellers have in placing regular orders with dozens of publishers, and likewise the large number of small orders that publishers must fill. The jobber, who can cut down the total number of industry transactions on the 20% of the titles that account for 80% of the sales, has not been of much help in fulfilling orders for special interest of technical titles. An ambitious stab at providing a clearinghouse channel for special orders was Bookamatic, Inc.

Commencing at the dawn of 1973, this New York company hoped to both reduce the time in getting single order copies to the customer and at the same time to cut the cost of handling to a level that would make it profitable for all parties. Performing the role of the middleman, Bookamatic took all special order requests from booksellers, using special forms designed to speed computer processing. Bookamatic then grouped orders by publishers, sending each a packing list and shipping documents, so that it could drop-ship directly to the stores. Bookamatic handled all the paperwork, sending each bookseller a consolidated monthly invoice. The firm hoped to get cooperation from publishers in the form of a 50% discount on books, while giving the retailer a 35% discount. In fact, the industry's resistance to change seems to have predominated, with a few publishers giving as much as 47% off, but some charging full list price. Speed of delivery was still up to the publishers' own fulfillment operations. Both publishers and booksellers often refused to use the special forms. However, a number of bookstores did find that the system was beginning to make single copy orders worthwhile — including Dalton, which has continued taking such requests on its own with a procedure based on Bookamatic's.

Although Bookamatic failed, in part, through publisher apathy, it did prove several points during its brief lifetime. Most importantly, it showed that booksellers can make money on special orders — and that it is a function that has untapped potential for exploitation. It got Dalton involved in special orders. The small number of individually owned stores that participated found that they could increase their business and profits with the system. Bookamatic also evolved into a small publisher fulfillment service. Stackpole Books, a small house that gave Bookamatic 50% off list, began turning over to it all the small orders that it found unprofitable to handle, since these involved relatively higher handling costs.

Although Bookamatic may have been ahead of its time, its near success, despite considerable institutional obstacles, should prove encouraging to some subsequent entrepreneurs who can fulfill the special order need in this manner.

At the other end of the business spectrum, it should not be surprising if mighty Baker & Taylor Co. leaps into the special order vacuum. The fit is right. First, B&T has the large inventory that would make it not only a paperprocessing clearinghouse but an actual depository for most of the books. Its warehouses carry as many as 110,000 titles at any time. Second, as the major library jobber, B&T already has the systems designed to process orders for single copies of many titles. Overall, its average number of copies per title per order is barely above one. Third, it has the financial wherewithal to make the modifications to its system and sustain the start-up costs of such an endeavor. Furthermore, if B&T must backorder those titles that it does not have, its position in the industry will carry more clout than little Bookamatic vis-à-vis the publishers.

Ingram is also contemplating such a service, but its resources are already strained in expanding its jobber operation. Other jobbers are certainly in a position to put together a special order package, but B&T is no doubt closest to having anything that could work from the start. The drawback to being so large, however, is that it may not want to deal with what may look like small potatoes compared to its other business. No doubt some good market research must not only digest the current volume of special order business but what the potential would be should it become soundly profitable to booksellers. It could add another major dimension to retailing books resulting in more sales, and partially solve the dilemma of how to best make use of the great number of titles in print.

HOW A BOOKSELLER BUYS

Chapter V outlined how publishers and jobbers sell. Faced with a blizzard of publishers' representatives, commission salesmen, catalogues, direct mailings, advertisements, and book reviews of hardcovers, trade and mass market paperbacks, just how does the bookseller make the decision on what to buy and how much? Simple. Talk to a dozen retailers and the responses will contain a dozen unique formulas. However, they are reduced to ten criteria, though the order of priority shifts according to the respondent.

● What is the book about? History may be in this year, biography out. For a while, anything on Watergate looked good.

● How much does it cost? Many booksellers are becoming increasingly concerned at the escalating cost of hardcover books. In mass market paper, they look askance at a price beyond the new $2.25 barrier.

● Who is the publisher? Reputation is more important for the bookseller than the consumer, but it helps in judging the quality of the work, as well as the fulfillment potential for reorders.

● What other books are there on the subject? The eighth book of the year on backgammon is not going to look as good as the first two.

● What is the first printing? To a large extent, this shows the publisher's commitment and expectation. The salesman may bally-hoo the title to the sky, but a first printing of 4000 is a telltale sign. It also ties in with . . .

● What are the planned advertising and promotion budgets? An author lined up for the national talk shows and big dollars for the book review media are big plusses.

● How timely is it? This supplements the first and the fourth item.

● Who is the author? For a few books this could be a major factor. An Arthur Hailey book may sell strongly regardless of the other factors, a James Michener title indicates a certain reliability. The mass market paperback western and romance originals have their own best selling writers, such as Bantam's Louis L'Amour. First book? Well, every author had to have one.

• Has the book been reviewed and what was the reaction? Sometimes reviews are too late to help the seller make initial decisions, but the advance review media, such as *Publisher's Weekly* forecasts, can provide guidelines. An interesting study for the future may be to correlate reviews with actual sales.

• What is the status of subsidiary rights? The selection by a major book club, or the sale of film rights, makes a big splash. In ordering the paperback print rights, the track record of the hardcover and the timing of any movie opening could be factored in.

Buying backlist titles is, naturally, a less risky decision, the major question being how many copies to put in inventory. Current trends in book purchases include a wariness of hardcover fiction, simply because it is not selling at $7.95 or $8.95. Not surprisingly, buying today includes a greater percentage of paperbacks. At Brentano's, paper has increased from 24% of stock in 1970 to a third by the beginning of 1975. Walden and B. Dalton both cite paperbacks as a growing percentage of their sales.

CONCLUSIONS

Some may protest otherwise, but bookselling is not a profession. It is a business, a retail business, with many of the same characteristics of any other retail operation. It has its unique problems, many of them stemming from the vast quantities of product with which stores must deal. As a retail business with a distinctive perfume, bookselling has attracted a certain type of entrepreneur, one who may love his work, but who in the aggregate does not maximize the sale of books.

The interest of big money in bookselling is doubly encouraging. It is good for the industry in that these chain operations mean a greater coverage of the marketplace with retail outlets, a recommendation that is at least as old as the 1931 Cheney Report. If retail stores are to provide time and place utility, there must be outlets, and they must be where people live or work. They must also carry a reasonable inventory and be prepared to acquire goods that are requested, but that they do not carry, in an expeditious manner. Chain stores generally, B. Dalton in particular, as well as the new single unit book merchandisers such as Preston Books in Dallas, are providing the place utility; the broader their inventories, the more likely they are to have a book when the customer wants it. Still to be improved on, however, is the special order situation. Bookamatic at least had a program that responded to what needed to be done and another system will no doubt surface to pick up where it left off. The big library jobbers are another possible solution. They certainly have the inventory and technology, so it is a matter of working out the economics and establishing the desire.

The interest of Carter Hawley Hale and Dayton Hudson in the book business is also encouraging because it should be good and welcome evidence that retail bookselling can be profitable. These companies have been expanding their chains for as long as ten years and they are still going strong. Hence, having seen the results, they are encouraged to continue and this should have the same impetus for independent booksellers to grow, add branches, and gain some of the multiunit economies for themselves. These booksellers can also take heart in the practicalities of special interest bookstores. Whereas in many trades subspecialty shops suffer from lack of merchandise, the bookselling community is cursed — or blessed — with an abundance of selections in almost any subject. This is one approach to narrowing the inventory problem, as well as a means to zero in on identifiable market segments.

X

Promotion, Advertising and Market Research

Book publishers and booksellers are not known for their overpowering advertising: they rarely buy time on television, have no singers crooning jingles on the radio, and their newspaper advertising is limited to a few Sunday sections and a few daily papers with large circulations. Certain consumer magazines carry a scattering of advertising messages, but not with any lingering sense of impact. Only the trade press can make a living from publishers' advertising, but even here there is but a handful of vehicles, *Publisher's Weekly* and *Library Journal* being the principal ones.

Nor has the publishing industry kept many market research firms busy at their calculators. The dearth of substantive investigation on book pricing, packaging, or subject matter is a scandal that only a few recognize, but no one seems willing to take any steps to improve.

Instead, publishers concentrate on a few tried and true promotional activities that keep publicity departments and outside flacks busy: author tours and autograph parties; appearances on the David Susskind, Johnny Carson, or "Today" shows; and book review copies by the dozens or hundreds.

The results? Well, John Wanamaker said it all when he mused about which half of his advertising dollar was being wasted. But in the book industry, there are not many advertising dollars being spent and even less money goes to determine which of these are the most effective.

This is not to suggest that there are no good reasons for the industry's relative lack of expenditure on advertising. Although "book" and "toothpaste" are each generic names for a classification of products, promoting a specific book is far different from promoting a specific toothpaste. The toothpaste equivalent would be if Lever Bros. came out with a different brand each month, changing the flavor, packaging, and price, with each new brand having a maximum potential sale to only 4% of the adult population. Under such circumstances, how much pretesting could Lever Bros. afford each month and how big an advertising push would be feasible? This is the situation facing publishers and booksellers, but it is one that they have not come to grips with yet as an industry, though there are some signs of movement.

No book publisher alone appears on *Advertising Age*'s list of 100 top advertisers for 1976, but the entire industry spent about $45 million in newspaper and magazine advertising and another $7-8 million on other media. Table X-1 compares aggregate promotional expenditures for different types of general book publishing. Measured media spending for trade book divisions alone are frightfully small, typically 2%-4% of total sales. In 1976, Table X-2 shows that Doubleday was the media expenditure leader, spending almost $10 million on its book clubs and another $1.2 million on its trade line. Among trade publishers alone, Encyclopaedia Britannica was the leader, spending $4.3 million. Random House; Harlequin; Little, Brown; and Dell (now part of Doubleday) also had expenditures above $1 million.

TABLE X-1:   Publisher Marketing Costs as a Percentage of Sales, 1976

Type of publisher	Advertising publicity, promotion expense	Selling expense	Total
Trade	9.0%	6.9%	15.9%
Professional	19.7	4.3	24.0
Mass market paperback[1]	2.9	5.8	8.7

[1] Figures are not strictly comparable because of differences in reporting.

SOURCE: Association of American Publishers, *Industry Statistics, 1976.* See also, Dinoo J. Vanier, *Market Structure and the Business of Book Publishing* (New York, Pitman Publishing, 1973), p. 156.

MARKETING RESEARCH

Although the choice of spending a minimum of $25,000 to market test a given book before publication is clearly out of the question, certain types of research are still practical for publishers. For example, market research can be used by a publisher to help determine what subject areas are ripe for new titles, what market within the subject category is most promising, and what the best channels of distribution might be for these titles. Chilton Book Company has based much of its new title output on just such in-house research. Through surveys, Chilton has come up with topics for its crafts and hobbies books, enabling the publisher to create a series of books that start at the beginner level. A coupon in the first book on stained glass includes a mail order coupon for a more advanced book. Chilton has also found that crafts shops, as well as bookstores, are a logical outlet for its wares. As a result, it can search for an author, commission a book, and actually be able to predict with some accuracy the level of sales. Rather than depending on speculation, Chilton only publishes what its research says will have a large enough audience to succeed.

As detailed in Chapter VII, the structure of the mail order publishing business makes extensive prepublication research not only feasible but necessary. This type of study, as with the Chilton books, concentrates first on testing the editorial concept. A second area of research takes a given editorial product and screens various packaging, channeling, and pricing possibilities. Such an investment in research helps explain the surprise success of Oxmoor's *Jericho*, which sold 160,000 copies, not at reprint prices but at a full $39.95. Oxmoor was initially inclined to price the book at $24.95 with no test, but decided to put $700,000 into testing (and $2 million in the total marketing effort). Thirteen tests ran altogether: the first four tests considered the mailing package – size of the envelope and brochure, even the possibility of a first class postage letter. Then came nine price tests, ranging from the lowest acceptable price $19.95) to a top of $39.95. The best response was 3.9% at the bottom price, but Oxmoor preferred instead the 2.3% response at the top price, since it yielded more profit. Oxmoor claims that a sale of 25,000 copies would have been worthwhile (although this seems a bit unrealistic, since it

TABLE X-2:   Publishers' Advertising, 1976 (thousands)

	Trade	Newspapers & Magazines	Radio & TV	Total	Adv. As % of Trade Sales
1. Encyclopaedia Britannica (includes Praeger, Merriam Webster)	$ 20.9	$3,419.6	$ 899.2	$4,339.7	2.5%
2. Random House (includes Knopf, Pantheon, Vintage, Ballantine)	79.6	1,397.6	206.5	1,763.4	2.3
3. Harlequin	1.2	182.8	1,109.1	1,293.1	2.4
4. Doubleday	51.3	1,167.1	–	1,218.4	2.6
5. Little, Brown	43.4	1,050.6	–	1,094.0	5.4
6. Dell (includes Delacorte, Dial)	58.7	826.1	172.8	1,057.5	1.5
7. Simon & Schuster (includes Pocket Books)	58.2	563.3	254.1	875.6	1.2
8. CBS/Holt, Rinehart & Winston, Popular Library	40.2	535.3	195.1	770.6	3.8
9. Avon	66.9	278.5	378.9	724.3	2.0
10. Macmillan	53.6	596.6	21.9	672.1	3.4
11. Harper & Row	51.1	567.3	–	662.6	2.4
12. Harcourt Brace Jovanovich (includes Pyramid, Pillar)	57.2	371.5	179.6	608.4	2.0
13. Bantam	41.8	273.6	279.7	595.1	0.7
14. Quadrangle/N.Y. Times	1.5	552.0	38.9	592.5	14.8
15. Putnam's (includes Coward McCann, Berkley)	115.6	376.2	36.1	527.9	2.4
16. Fawcett	38.2	354.4	73.9	466.5	0.9
17. William Morrow	46.3	419.2	–	465.5	3.3
18. Houghton Mifflin	36.2	404.6	–	440.8	3.3
19. Viking/Penguin	47.4	355.4	–	402.8	2.0
20. Field Enterprises/World Book	–	375.4	–	375.4	0.2

Book Club and Mail Order Advertising, 1976

	Newspapers & Magazines	Radio & TV	Total	Adv. As % of Sales
1. Doubleday	$9,714.2	$ 50.0	$9,764.2	9.3%
2. Time-Life Books	7,955.3	909.6	8,864.9	7.9
3. Book-of-the-Month Club	4,729.7	—	4,729.7	7.4
4. Reader's Digest Books	3,498.2	12.5	3,510.7	4.7
5. Grolier Enterprises	1,197.8	668.2	1,862.7	2.6

SOURCE: *BP Report*, May 30, 1977, Knowledge Industry Publications, Inc.

would bring in under $1 million, leaving only $300,000 for production, handling, overhead and profit). In fact, the publisher wound up selling 100,000 copies through a direct mailing of 6.5 million pieces, 11,000 copies through print advertising, and the rest through bookstores.

Where does this leave the publishers of ordinary $6.95 novels, $12.50 biographies, and $2.25 mass market reprints? Major publishers can follow the Chilton example and explore needs for titles in specific areas, rather than wait for a book to catch on and then quickly try to follow up the competition with a mimicking title (witness the rush in 1975 into transcendental meditation and quilt making). They can also use existing data to explore which segments of the book-buying population are buying what types of books, as well as the geographical differences in sales. Some of this is already being done, e.g., the paperback houses and IDs who are basing their distribution on regional and store buying patterns.

Book covers are known to influence book buying. Most cover selections are now made by editors and designers, usually with input from salesmen. Two or more alternative covers will be drawn up, but the decision on which to use is made mostly by feel. Instead, consumer panels could be used to test responses to alternative covers for titles, testing the covers for a future month's releases in one sitting. The research design for this type of testing is relatively simple, well understood, and inexpensive. And with a group of covers being tested at a time, the cost can be amortized over the lot, making such tests practical for paperbacks as well.

Oscar Dystel, Bantam's sagacious chief executive, has asserted that pricing a mass market book at $2.25 cuts its initial draw by 25% over the same book at $1.95. This may be, but no one knows for sure. Again, constructing a series of tests in several markets, controlling for all variables except price, would help answer this question. Perhaps the price ceiling holds for some classifications of books more than others. Bantam, Avon, Dell, and Fawcett each should have the resources, and the interest, to pursue such research.

The Association of American Publishers has recently established a marketing committee that is beginning to address itself, however gingerly, to these matters. One brief study, conducted by Doubleday with the AAP, looked at the importance of dust jackets — and found that they are indeed necessary. Another project was to look into the returns situation, but, as described, it was more an examination of existing policies than market research involving booksellers. Possibly the most ambitious program from this committee was the "Books as Gifts" TV advertising experiment first scheduled for the Christmas 1975 selling season but later delayed until 1976. It was to employ selected test markets coupled with a book purchase attitude study. Although there are legal considerations in joint publisher endeavors, the AAP is the logical focus for such efforts. Giants Doubleday and McGraw-Hill are two of the most active researchers, both with full-time departments that monitor book sales after each advertising push. Most other publishers can only measure order volume, a less precise guide because it gauges retailer, not consumer, response.

There is also a paucity of knowledge about book buyer behavior. The American Booksellers Association has been quite active in its educational programs for booksellers, but its statistical base of information is just being developed. Although the available evidence seems to support such contentions as the spontaneous nature of many book purchases, it is axiomatic that in order to broaden the market for a product — and books are a product — a firm or industry must be able to identify various segments of the market, the motivations for use of the product by each segment, and the best way of reaching them. Chains such as Walden and Dalton intuitively know to locate stores in affluent suburban malls, but even they are using gut feelings, rules of thumb, and some past experiences in determining the mix of book subjects and formats in their stores, although Walden has done some testing of alternative advertising packages. The question "Who buys books?" has been answered. But many others are left: How can we reach those who are not buying books — both those with the same characteristics of book buyers (education and income), as well as those with differing characteristics? In what ways are book buyers and non-buyers with similar educational background different? What media are most effective in promoting which types of books to which audiences? What are the variables of price, cover design, size, and format? Is there any recognition of or loyalty to a publisher's imprint by consumers? Designing studies to respond to these questions can be left to the larger publishers and the trade associations, but there is an opportunity for market research firms looking to open up new markets for their own services.

Publishers and booksellers use five major methods in getting their books to the stores and sold to consumers: advertising; book reviews; publicity; point-of-sale merchandising; personal sales. This last involves the activity of publishers' representatives in selling their lines to book retailers and has already been discussed in Chapter V.

ADVERTISING

Advertising takes three forms: publishers' trade advertising, publishers' consumer advertising, and booksellers' consumer advertising. The most concentrated advertising is that which the publishers schedule to promote their new titles or new editions to the trade. Frequently this takes the form of multipage spreads in *Publisher's Weekly*, with the big Spring and Fall announcement issues running into the hundreds of pages. Similar ads are run for librarians in *Library Journal, The Booklist,* and *Wilson Library Bulletin.* Paperback houses now run ads in the Council for Periodical Distributors Association newsletter. Publishers may also pay jobbers, such as Ingram or Baker & Taylor, to promote their books in mailings and brochures. Most publishers also put together catalogues, featuring new books as well as the most popular backlist titles. These are often sent to educational institutions in addition to booksellers.

Trade and consumer

It is hard to judge the effectiveness of trade advertising – there have been no reports of serious attempts to take such measurements, other than the 1974 AAP/ALA study which found that direct mail pieces were more highly favored than catalogues among librarians. The ostensible objectives are to make the trade aware of what the publishers have to offer, so that the bookseller or librarian will order the book or be more receptive when the salesman calls. Trade ads also provide information on the consumer promotion plans the publisher might have, as well as quotes from reviews, if available — and favorable. Nonetheless, all but the most dedicated buyers are swamped by this media blitz, especially the announcements issues, where page after page of gray copy ballyhooing this title or that backlist must surely discourage even the bravest bookseller.

Publisher advertising to the consumer, other than the huge direct mail packages of Time-Life Books and others, has heretofore been concentrated in print media. The bulk of the advertising dollars goes into the *New York Times Book Review* section and the *New York Review of Books*. Lesser amounts are focused on the Sunday book review pages of the few major newspapers that devote space to this purpose. The other major media have been the literary and intellectual magazines: *Harper's, New Republic, Commentary*, et al. In almost every case, the ads are small and promote a single title.

Booksellers have generally restricted their meager advertising budgets to displays in the Yellow Pages and some cooperative ads with publishers in the newspapers. What these traditional approaches have in common is that all are aimed at the current book buyer and reader. Although this is the obvious place to begin, it is nonetheless limiting, since the future of bookselling lies in broadening the market. Publishers and to a lesser extent retailers have begun testing the broadcast media waters, as well as trying new forms of print advertising. The returns have been encouraging enough to stimulate greater interest in these media.

Perhaps the cheapest and most logical changes merely involve where advertisements in the newspapers are placed. Mass market paperback houses are now putting ads for certain titles on the women's pages or in general news pages. Bantam tried using this approach for the widely appealing *Plantation*. If these books are supposed to be mass market, obviously they should be promoted to a wider audience. Other publishers try the sports or business pages for appropriate titles.

Television

Bolder and much more expensive is advertising on television. It is clear from the financial realities of publishing that few books can be efficiently promoted through this medium. In 1976, book publishing houses spent $5.5 million on television and radio, which itself was 156% above the 1972 total, indicating that after some brief, though delayed, testing of the waters, the publishing industry has now taken the plunge.

There are some in the industry who insist — with little to support them — that people do not buy books on impulse. Marian Young, the media director at Sussman & Sugar Advertising, a book specialist agency, hypothesizes, "Buying a book is a deliberate process, and most people won't make the investment on the basis of a 30-second spot." Robin Smith, president of the Doubleday Book Clubs, shares this view. The little data gathered to date suggest that television is more useful for some types of books than others. The Bantam Books test for the paperback edition of Jacqueline Susann's *Once Is Not Enough* was inconclusive enough to lead Bantam to postpone further ads for the book, since Bantam could not in fact tell if its television campaign was increasing sales. Doubleday's push on television for Rose Kennedy's *Times to Remember* resulted first in rising sales, but a follow-up campaign several weeks later was not very successful.

Television is ideally suited for bringing a visual excitement to books through its use of movement, sound, and color. Its greatest returns are in informing many people quickly about a new product. Houghton Mifflin found this to be the case in promoting its *American Heritage Dictionary*, a "cool" product if ever there was one. Dictionaries are one of the most commonly owned of all books, and since they are a relatively high ticket item, Houghton Mifflin was able to justify the rare use of network television. Houghton has used the "Today," "Tonight," and Dick Cavett shows over the years (starting in 1969), having the announcers do the commercial live, which saves much money on production costs. The big difficulty in using television is that the book needs a saturation campaign and continuity over a period of time, which makes it more adaptable to a reference work than a bestseller.

Warner Paperback Library has made extensive use of television, running attention-getting 30-second spots to create interest in books as different as *All the President's Men* and *Sybil*. Warner claims to have spent over $1 million on television in 1975 to promote five books. The ads were aired only in selected markets. Even with such blockbuster titles, the economics of television advertising is formidable: if a publisher grosses 50% of the cover price, that becomes $.975 of a $1.95 book. Half of that goes to manufacturing and royalties, leaving less than $.49 for selling, overhead, and promotion. If Warner spent $1 million for five books, or $200,000 per title, the ad campaign came out to a substantial $.10 per book *if* 2 million copies are sold. To be more sound in the analysis, the real criteria are the *marginal* sales of the book. That is, titles such as *The Camerons* or *The War Between the Tates* would sell soundly with no or minimal traditional advertising. Warner must judge its real ad cost per book based on the additional copies sold attributable to the TV campaign. The true figures to measure, then, are what part of the $1 million went into television (the marginal cost) and what additional sales (marginal revenue) did it produce? Such calculations are difficult to make in the absence of test markets and control markets, which is what separates selling a specific book title from a bar of soap. In 1976, Warner's TV and radio expenditures were down to about $150,000.

There have been some attempts to test television effectiveness. Several years ago, an inexpensive 30-second spot commercial for the $1.95 paperback of Jose Torres' book on Muhammad Ali *Sting Like a Bee* was used in St. Louis. Without the TV spots, a sale of 450 copies was predicted. The ensuing campaign consisted of only six airings of the commercial in a one week period. Over 3800 copies of the book were sold within 20 days, at an ad cost of $1500. In this case, the television spots just about broke even (Table X-3), but did demonstrate television's impact as a stimulus on sales.

Needless to say, in the long run a publisher would want to do better than break even. Further experiments should consider such items as whether doubling the number of spots (which would not double the cost) could more than double the sale of books. In 1976, Harlequin was the leading publisher in TV and radio advertising expenditures, with a reported $1.1 million spent to promote its romance titles.

Booksellers have even more difficulty in using television, which is not known as a strong or economical medium for retail trade generally. There are some exceptions, however. Mills Bookstore, an established Nashville, Tennessee, dealer, found that it was

TABLE X-3:   Estimated Analysis of Marginal Cost and Revenue for
St. Louis TV Test

Actual sales	3869 copies	Marginal revenue	
Predicted sales		(97.5¢ x 3419)	$3,334
without TV	450 copies		
		Less:	
Marginal sales	3419 copies	Manufacturing and	
		royalty cost	1,667
			$1,667
		Cost of 6 spots $1500	
		Creative cost $ 300	
		Total campaign expense	1,800
		Net gain (loss) on	
		ad campaign	($ 133)

profitable to buy five minutes every other week on a popular local midday talk show. During this time owner Bernard Schweid and the show's host would discuss two books, hitting points on the plot and what sort of reader would like the book. Today he has a five minute segment every other week, often with an author as guest. As a nonpaid part of the show, his bookstore is not named, but many books do sell naturally better after a mention on the program. After Schweid's first appearance on the show the store had sold a dozen books before he had even gotten back from the studio. The format is obviously important. It is not a spot for the bookstore *per se*, nor is it a hard sell for a book. Working from the success that authors have in selling their books just from being invited onto the popular talk shows, the store's original commercials were structured to blend into the program's format. No doubt it also sold copies of the book at other stores, but that is why the publishers paid a cooperative share. Mills finds that television is best suited for selling nonfiction, self-help, and how-to books; occasionally some popular fiction. "Literary books" go nowhere on television, he reports.

B. Dalton has not yet found itself able to justify much use of television but Waldenbooks has been using the medium for several years, primarily during the Christmas season. The Walden TV approach is part of a total media package that also uses radio but relies most heavily on newspapers. The Walden television spots favor time during the "Today" show, but they are also run at other times during adult viewing hours to reach people who don't ordinarily buy books. During the 1973 season, for example, Walden had author George Plimpton make 45 30-second commercials, each featuring two books. These were run six to ten times each in 12 cities where Walden had a large enough concentration of stores. Publishers paid 75% of the $425,000 cost through co-operative allowances.

Walden has based its total campaign, called Mediamix because of the TV/radio/newspaper combination it uses, on results of a preliminary test in 1972. In the test, sales were compared on key books in areas where the media mix was run and where it was not run. Walden concluded that some books did best in newspaper ads and that radio often elicited a better response than anticipated. The test also convinced Walden to cut the number of books covered in each television commercial to a pair.

Television has been used to a limited degree by the book clubs and direct mail publishers. Book-of-the-Month Club tried to get new members through an experimental use of TV but did not find it very effective. It tried a second time, using an 800 toll-free number. Literary Guild has been somewhat more aggressive and has been "moderately encouraged" but sees its use of television only as a supplement to print. "Since broadcast involves a finite amount of time, we have to offer things that have a higher identification quantity," explains a Literary Guild executive. It is not a significant part of either club's budget. Time-Life Books has been using 120-second spots during late night and early morning "fringe hour" periods, making the same pitch as in the direct mail pieces. The ads offer both a mail address and a toll-free phone number. Meredith has taken some spots for its *Golden Treasury of Cooking* on the "Today" show, as much to aid bookstore sales as to get direct mail orders.

The big obstacle to this use of television is the "conversion" problem. Even if the customer calls — the best outcome — he must be sent an agreement form to sign and at this point there is a fall off. At least one of the clubs also finds that television brings in the wrong people, i.e., those who are more prone to fulfilling only their minimum commitment, or worse, taking the four for $1 and then fading away.

Taking a leaf from the florists, the marketing committee of AAP's General Publishing Division has come up with a pilot program for an institutional television campaign with a "A Book is a Living Gift" theme. The commercials show people receiving books as gifts — and being just thrilled about it. The initial plan was for an expenditure of $200,000 in 1976 spent during the Christmas season, to be financed through added dues assessments to AAP members. As for the impact of the commercials, in the two test cities, results indicated a modest improvement compared to two control group cities.

The idea of using a theme that popularizes books is certainly a movement in the right direction. As committee co-chairman Roger Straus III explained to the AAP's Fifth Annual Meeting, the idea is "to get away from the 'vitamin' approach — the elitist notion that you should buy books because they're good for you. That drives people away." The budget was doubled for 1977, but the program was dropped in 1978 due to differences of opinion within the AAP membership on its implementation.

Radio and posters

Radio has proven to have its best effects when it is used as a reinforcement to television or print, although it requires frequent repetition of the message. Houghton Mifflin has supplemented its dictionary TV campaign with radio at Christmas time, even giving retailers in selected cities free tag lines. The "American Heritage" ads were ad-libbed by announcers, using information from a fact sheet, a technique that gets the announcers (such as New York's John Gambling or comedians Bob and Ray) more involved in the subject and sometimes results in free additional air time. Houghton Mifflin, as well as media specialists, feel that radio is most effective with products that are already known and favors buying drive time (rush hour) or using shows that have large and loyal audiences. However, individual titles can be looked at more closely for a logical audience (a book on the Beatles could find its place on an FM "progressive" music station).

Radio has the advantage of being highly localized so that

choosing stations or programs carefully, audience segments can be identified. Moreover, it is relatively inexpensive: a full week of spots on three major New York radio stations costs about the same as a single page in the *New York Times Book Review* section. Although Walden uses radio as part of its Mediamix, its most recent evaluation is that it is only successful for "the individual title that is tailored to an individual station and audience." B. Dalton's Pickwick Stores, however, have found that with 68% of the adult population of Los Angeles on the road in the morning, radio can be quite effective.

A medium new to book publishing is mass transit. One firm, Transportation Display Incorporated, arranges for advertising on suburban railroads, airports, and terminals. Bantam, Warner, and a few others have promoted some titles through subway posters in several cities. Clearly limited to the most mass marketable of titles, this approach does attempt to reach beyond the usual book-buying milieu. Such posters offer the attraction of continuous exposure, as much as twice a day and 44 rides a month if blanketed over the transit system. It too awaits market testing to establish its cost effectiveness.

Print and co-op

The print media, however, will remain the prime channel for the industry's advertising. Through the selective use of magazines and newspapers, publishers can most accurately communicate to the mainstay of the market — the current bookbuyers — yet can reach out to those who are the most likely potential readers for their books. Trade and professional books in particular must depend on this focus to make efficient use of their advertising dollars. Publishers still depend on print to reinforce their television images. The AAP Books as Gifts campaign uses the same people and story lines in print ads as in the television spots.

For booksellers, there is no real alternative to print as the mainstay of their advertising. Even Walden has concluded that print is the most important vehicle with major metropolitan newspapers the best of all, supplemented by suburban "shoppers."

Most publishers use cooperative advertising to some degree.

Although details vary, a publisher will offer to pay as much as 75% of the retailer's space or time expense for advertising selected books. The total sum available to any retailer from any publisher is typically limited to 5% or 10% of the retailer's net purchases from the publisher for the previous calendar year. Thus, a bookseller who has spent $3000 with Macmillan one year has available $300 to advertise current Macmillan titles. Since the retailer must contribute 25%, a single ad costing $400 would use up the cooperative allowance from Macmillan for the year. Other publishers allow 10% of the net price for a given order of books. The publishers generally supply newspaper mats or paste-ups for print media, many also provide radio spots for a title or two. In either case, the bookseller gets to put the name and address of the store(s) at the bottom or end of the ad. In many instances cooperative money can be used toward catalogues, sample copies of books, store displays, or autographing parties.

One of the sources of resistance that wholesalers and jobbers have encountered in signing up bookstores as accounts stems from the fact that retailers have difficulty getting credit from publishers for co-op money on purchases channeled through the wholesaler. Such purchases involve the added paperwork of providing the publisher with a statement of purchase, the name of the wholesaler, and other relevant information.

The chain operations lean heavily on publishers for cooperative funds, as Walden's pre-Christmas Mediamix expenditures make evident. Brentano's, however, has changed the nature of its print. At one time it was running 250,000 lines in the *New York Times*, pushing popular hardcover titles and collecting co-op money for it. Now it shies away from such promotion, figuring that it did not pay to advertise the same bestseller that everyone sold at the same price. Instead Brentano's is buying 60,000 lines and concentrating on ads selling remainder titles or special titles that no one else is pushing, such as the full page spread in the *Wall Street Journal* (with a coupon) for a then obscure book called *Winning Through Intimidation*, at $9.95 plus postage. (Later the book climbed high on bestseller lists.)

There is at least one cynic in the industry who maintains that, in the absence of hard data, publisher advertising is not all that effective. A trade hardcover buyer for a major retail chain, she feels that publishers advertise for four reasons: 1) to impress agents; 2) to calm authors, who like to see their names in the media and want to be sure the publisher is doing its utmost for his or her book; 3) to get a higher paperback rights price; 4) least importantly, as a serious means to sell the book. Such a jaundiced view is based in some part in reality. There are reports now and then of a publisher continuing an intensive ad campaign to maintain a book on the bestseller list while negotiating film or reprint rights. (Of course, a film producer might also contribute to a publisher's advertising fund to sustain interest in anticipation of a film's release). Publishers know that authors prefer to submit manuscripts to companies that are generous with their advertising support. Thus, advertising helps attract both new and established authors. Another purpose of advertising is to create interest on the part of book reviewers, making them more likely to schedule that title for review.

The irony of advertising budgets is that they are based on a book's expected sale. Thus, expected bestsellers are blessed with multi-thousand dollar budgets, whereas first novels, no matter how good, rarely are heard from again for lacc of promotion. Occasionally a *Jonathan Livangston Seagull* will get the spark on its own and once it takes off the promotional coffers open up. It's hard to imagine how else it could work, since publishers can't commit large sums to unknown books. Still, the idea persists that if advertising means anything at all, it should be able to improve sales of any book that is worth publishing.

BOOK REVIEWS, PUBLICITY, AND MERCHANDISING

Publicity, unlike advertising, is unpaid-for information presented about the book, author, or subject. To be sure, many publishers spend large sums on publicity departments to help get these "free" mentions, but it is misleading to figure they might just as well put their PR budget into advertising instead. Consumers are overwhelmed with and cynical about advertising. Hence, favorable information about a product that comes from a supposedly independent source is considered more valuable than paid ads. The frequent payola scandals in the record industry are a case in point. Promotion people would rather pay off disc jockeys to spin their songs as legitimate plays than spend the same money on acknowledged 60-second plugs.

Reviews

One of the most sought after forms of publicity in book publishing are reviews. For most titles, perhaps 100 free copies are sent to appropriate reviewers; special interest and academic books have the best chance of having a review printed in magazines or scholarly journals for that interest or discipline. Unfortunately, these reviews often appear months, and in the case of scholarly journals, years, after the book's publication. Until recently, few reviewing media paid attention to any original publication appearing only in paperback, but that is slowly changing, with the *New York Times Book Review* devoting a separate section and listing for both mass market and trade paperbacks.

The number of general consumer book review media can be counted on one hand: *The New York Times Book Review*, the new *West Coast Review of Books,* and the *New York Review of Books.* Far behind is *Saturday Review.* Small circulation intellectual journals, among them *Nation, National Review,* and *New Republic,* are able to mention several books in each weekly or monthly issue. *Time* and *Newsweek,* the most widely circulated magazines that carry regular book reviews, can write up a maximum of four or five books a week. The book review supplement of the Sunday Washington *Post* folded as a separate publication in 1973, though it continues within the paper. *Harper's Magazine* was not able to make a success of *Bookletter*, a biweekly consumer newsletter that critiqued about a dozen major titles plus another half dozen lumped within a separate article. It also provided a mail order service for books reviewed or advertised.

Given this paucity of consumer reviewing media the vast majority of general books never get reviewed at all for a general audience — volume is against them. In 1976, 26,983 new titles were issued. Of these, 6155 were classified as fiction, general reference, literature, poetry/drama, or biography, the subjects most likely to warrant general consumer reviews. But the largest of the consumer book review media, *The New York Times Book*

Review, was able to deal with only 1012 titles, plus an additional 174 of the 2039 juvenile titles issued that year. In fact, *The Times* decreased the number of books reviewed in 1976 more than 10% from 1975. Included in its totals are dozens of books mentioned only in passing in such columns as "Criminals at Large."

Most of the other book review media listed in Table X-4, are trade publications, providing information for librarians, teachers, and booksellers. These cover a far larger volume of books than *The Times* or other consumer media. Still, the combined total of all reviews in all the major media, trade and consumer, was 31,683 in 1976. So even if each review were not duplicated (which is far from actual practice), they would just barely cover the field.

Thus, there is great competition for reviewer notice. Some books will get the attention automatically: successful authors, politicians, controversial people, or entertainers. Thus, first authors and the less well established must maneuver for the room that is left. Publishers are often as concerned with the short reviews in the trade magazines, since these appear in advance of publication and no review (or maybe even worse, a bad notice), lessens the chance of the book's even being ordered by a bookseller or library. On the other hand, a few good words can be exploited in advertising blurbs and promotion pieces. Sometimes publishers are successful in getting reviews in nonbook media. A "crock pot" cookbook sent to newspaper food writers might get a column or a mention just as sports books are sometimes picked up by sports columnists.

Author tours are another way of attracting review attention as well as gaining other publicity as the writer makes him or herself available for interviews with the press in major book buying cities. Usually, when a publisher is willing to spend the time and money for such tours review attention is already assured, but additional local publicity may ensue. Publishers also throw cocktail parties or lavish soirees to gain added attention, with one of the most elaborate of the latter being a bash hosted by Harper & Row in 1975. The black-tie affair, coinciding with the ABA's 75th anniversary convention in New York, brought thousands to mark the publication of a new biography of Judy Garland, one of several being published by different houses almost simultaneously.

How effective reviews are in selling books is highly debatable.

TABLE X-4: Number of Books Reviewed by Major Book-Reviewing Publications, 1975 and 1976

Publication	Adult 1976	Adult 1975	Juvenile 1976	Juvenile 1975	Young Adult 1976	Young Adult 1975	Total 1976	Total 1975
Booklist	3,014	2,178	1,109	844	277	1,176	4,719[1]	4,218[1]
Bulletin of the Center for Children's Books	—	—	425	435	373	378	798	813
Choice	6,402	6,583	—	—	—	—	6,402	6,583
Horn Book	—	55	397	375	32	—	429	430
Kirkus Services	2,825	2,939	1,225	1,321	—	—	4,050	4,260
Library Journal	5,819	6,149	—	—	—	—	5,819	6,149
New York Review of Books	308	385	6	—	—	—	314	385
New York Times	1,012	1,058	174	174	—	—	1,186[2]	1,332[2]
Publisher's Weekly	3,666	3,334	518	483	—	—	4,184[3]	3,817[3]
School Library Journal	—	—	2,117	2,129	313	353	2,430	2,482
West Coast Review of Books	1,242	—	110	—	—	—	1,352	—

[1] Includes 319 reference and subscription books. In addition, Booklist published 908 reviews of nonprint materials.
[2] Includes major reviews of the Sunday Book Review, as well as the departments "For Young Readers" and "Criminals at Large."
[3] Includes reviews of paperback originals and reprints.

SOURCE: Bowker Annual of Library and Book Trade Information, 1977.

Examples are legion of lavishly praised books falling flat, and panned works becoming bestsellers. Popular novels by Arthur Hailey, the late Jacqueline Susann, and Harold Robbins have consistently sold regardless of the reviewers. A few years ago, *Time* said about Irving Stone's *Passions of the Mind*, "Eight hundred pages long and two inches thick, the book is an imposing object that should find many uses. It could serve, for instance, as a deadweight that could instantly sink a prosperous 68-year-old author into the East River." The book reached the top of the bestseller charts, as did a not quite so broadly attacked *Love Story*.

Publicity, author appearances

Better than reviews and tour publicity, the most sought after *coup* in the promotion bag is an author appearance on a television show to plug his book. The *crème de la crème* of these is an interview on the "Today" or "Tonight" shows, with Merv Griffin and Mike Douglas second best. Within the audiences for these shows are large proportions of book buyers, some who no doubt tune in for these interviews. Booksellers can point to almost immediate runs on books that have been mentioned on these shows. A typical phenomenon: after the author of an obscure book called *T.M.: Discovering Energy and Overcoming Stress* was interviewed on the "Tonight" show, bookstores were cleaned out and the surprised publisher, Delacorte, had to rush back to press as the book hit the bestseller list overnight. There was also a faddish fallout. Another TM title, in trade paperback, sold out its first printing of 10,000 in two days at the 1975 ABA show and postponed its publication date to do a 100,000 second printing.

Autograph parties are a method of stimulating local book sales as well as gaining press coverage. Usually as part of a tour, the author will spend an hour or two at a major bookstore or department store signing greetings in copies of his book bought at the time. This technique is the province almost exclusively of trade hardcover books. However, enterprising small retailers can make their own opportunities. When the owners of a new Elkins Park, Pennsylvania, bookstore heard that Marvin Kalb, one of the authors of *Kissinger*, was going to be speaking in the area, they got a quick supply of the books from a jobber, arranged for Kalb to sign books purchased by the audience, and sold 20 copies that evening.

Another tried-and-true publicity gambit is to piggyback onto a movie promotion. Whereas mass market paper reprints have long added stills from a successful movie to their editions, now reprinters are converting the original screen plays of successful movies and even television shows into books. These editions make use of the artwork, logos, and pictures from the movie for the cover tie-in. *The Sting* and *Young Frankenstein* are recent examples of this approach, as are several books generated by the ongoing British television series, "Upstairs, Downstairs." Other books are repackaged after the movie, using the film artwork, such as *The Taking of Pelham One Two Three* and *The Stepford Wives.*

Thus, reviews, television or radio appearances, publicity tours, autographing sessions, and movie tie-ins are all sources of promotion other than directly paid-for advertising.

Merchandising

Merchandising involves point-of-sale promotions, instruments that help sell a consumer once he or she is in a bookstore. The techniques used are window displays, streamers, posters, stickers, counter cards, dump bins, and bookmarks. They are used to stimulate recognition of a book learned about through an advertisement the previous Sunday or seen on television between gulps of coffee and a glance at the newspaper during breakfast two weeks earlier.

Paperbacks, both trade and mass market, are especially suitable for many of these tools. Dump bins are specially constructed cardboard units that contain a mass display of a particular book. Some publishers include a wire counter rack or display box with an order of a minimum size. Of course, here again every publisher is competing for the limited space a bookseller can devote to special displays or preferred counter space. Larger publishers rely on their sales representatives to encourage prime space for their displays. To inspire booksellers to take certain display racks, streamers, or bins, publishers will allow special promotional discounts of 2%-3% more than usual when the order is for a dump bin display or the equivalent. These special discounts are also used by about 15% of the publishers on a regular basis for selected titles, at trade shows or before a selling season. The hope is that with a greater margin, the bookseller will recommend these books more frequently or display them with greater prominence than otherwise.

For all books — but especially for paperbacks — the cover itself is a point-of-sale advertising tool, and choosing the right design (sometimes called "packaging" the paperback) is a decision of major import. For example, NAL's provocative cover for the mass market paperback of Erica Jong's *Fear of Flying* is widely credited with turning a moderately successful hardcover bestseller into a paperback sensation. First Bantam, with *Future Shock*, and later other paperback houses, have used the technique of printing the cover for an edition in several different colors and having these on sale side by side, providing still another device for catching the passerby's attention.

Merchandising techniques are most useful in stimulating sales of "blockbuster" paperbacks or those with some timely or faddish impact. They do not pull many people into the store, although an attractive store window can beckon to passersby. They do encourage the impulse purchase.

CONCLUSION

Book publishers and some sellers have been exploring new ways of using the media to both expand the audience for books and reach current buyers more efficiently. But the industry as a whole is still working in the dark, making many decisions based on experience, feelings, and tradition. These frequently work well, other times not so well; no one can know for sure whether the results they produce are optimal. The industry is too small to be able to engage in the large-scale research of the soap powder and mouthwash manufacturers, but there are procedures that are relatively inexpensive and can be applied by either individual firms or through the trade associations to better understand both the nature of their products and their consumers. Right now, only the mail order publishers are collecting this information systematically.

The book industry has not been terribly creative in its approach to advertising, but this too seems to be rapidly shifting. The major problem is that of multiplicity of titles, for even the largest selling books cannot justify the major promotional expenditures that other consumer products typically employ. In the long run, however, that may change. As the number of book outlets increases, institutional ad campaigns, working in congruence with ever rising educational levels, may result in a greater volume of books being sold. But this will hold only if publishers can control the increase in new titles so that sales per title would rise and there would be more money per title available for promotion. If instead of being able to sell an average of 20,000 copies of a moderately successful trade title or 400,000 copies for a mass market title, the average moves up by 20%, then the fixed costs become amortized over that many more books, leaving proportionally more for advertising and profit, which could start a cycle creating even more sales.

Advertising and promotion do not, for sure, exist apart from the distribution system. Encouraging consumers to purchase a title is self-defeating unless there are bookstores to carry them, a distribution network to get them into the store, or a workable special order procedure to get individual requests processed quickly. There is more than one story of an author on tour showing up for a well-publicized autographing session and finding that the supply of books the retailer ordered weeks ago hadn't yet arrived.

Advertising and promotion are part of the communication process that has the staggering job of informing millions of people about thousands of new products each month, no two of which are exactly alike. Under the best of conditions, communications do not always work smoothly between senders and receivers. In the case of the book industry, conditions are far from the best. Nonetheless, it is impressive how well and powerful such an archaic form called "word of mouth" often operates. Despite efforts of reviewers, publicists, authors, et al., many books, good and bad, are not commercial successes. Yet other titles, which may never get an official inauguration, struggle on their own and break out into the big time, solely through person-to-person recommendations: *Jonathan Livingston Seagull* languished above the tips of the waves for an extended period, then took off without the media. Tom Robbins, author of *Even Cowgirls Get the Blues*, sold hundreds of thousands of books for Bantam just on word of mouth. And how did the *Lord of the Rings* trilogy develop to the point where it merited a special package promotion?

Instances such as these sometimes confirm the cynical or smug judgment of publishers that things will be as they always have been in the book business, and that publishers can get along quite well without the marketing tools, or perhaps even the advertising budgets, of other industries. Yet what these successes point out is that fathoming public tastes in books is an unusually tricky and sophisticated job — one that, if anything, calls for more research and experimentation, not less. The most successful publishers are the most restless in looking for new possibilities. As one head of a paperback house put it: "What do we mean by a mass market anyway? Why did *The Godfather* sell 10 million copies? Why not 12 million? Or 15 million?" Struggling for some answers should push the book publishing industry into uncharted but not necessarily unprofitable territory.

XI

Education Markets for General Books

The sale of general books to school, college, and university outlets accounts for over a fourth of all sales of these books. For certain categories, education-related sales are an even more significant component of the sales mix. Tables XI-1 and XI-2 show the importance of general book sales within the education markets. Trade, professional, and university press publishers depend heavily on the use of their books in schools and colleges for their sales, with over half of the trade paperbound books being accounted for through this market. In fact, these sales comprise nearly 20% of all material sales in the el-hi market, and over 34% in the college market.

In el-hi, textbooks are barely 50% of materials expenditures, the remainder going for AV materials, general books, reference books, maps, and standardized tests. Combined with the estimated market for general books in libraries (Chapter VI), almost 50% of juvenile books as well as of all trade books are sold to these two markets. On the other hand, only 17% of the mass market paperbacks are sold to libraries or educational institutions.

Because of the already high penetration of general books in this market, combined with temporarily falling enrollments (Table III-11), this outlet does not appear very promising for expanding sales volume. Nonetheless there are specific opportunities for some segments of the publishing industry.

For example, although many college courses have long been using paperbound books instead of, or to supplement, textbooks, this practice is not as prevalent at the elementary and high school (el-hi) levels. As seen from Table XI-1, general books account for a considerably larger share of books bought at the college level than at the el-hi level. Mass market paperbacks, however, can look forward to mining both markets. Moreover, the unbroken rise in the level of educational attainment (Table XI-3) means that more people are staying in school longer, hence are using more books over the course of their formal education.

TABLE XI-1: Estimates for General Books Sold in Educational Markets, 1976 (millions of dollars)

	1976	
	El-hi (K-12)	College (13 up)
Trade, total	$ 79.4	$ 96.3
Adult Hardbound	31.3	45.2
Adult Paperbound	6.8	39.9
Juvenile	31.7	–
Religious	9.6	11.2
Professional, total	18.9	112.0
Technical & Scientific	6.4	42.1
Business & Other Professional	10.9	45.1
Medical	1.6	24.8
Book Clubs & Mail Order Publications	82.6	3.1
University Presses	1.6	19.0
Total, general	$ 182.5	$230.4
Mass Market Paperback	41.0	26.0
Total non-text sales	$ 223.5	$256.4
Total Market for Educational Materials	$1151.0	736.0
General and Mass Market Books as % of Total Market	19.4%	34.8%

SOURCE: Association of American Publishers, *Industry Statistics, 1976*, Table T2, plus estimates of Knowledge Industry Publications, Inc. for total market size.

SELLING TO EDUCATION MARKETS

Getting non-textbooks into the school and college classrooms requires a different set of skills and approaches than selling to bookstores and libraries. In the public schools, there are often district, systemwide, or state imposed restrictions on what titles can be bought, and in 22 states all books are listed or approved by a central state agency. Second, at all education levels, but particularly in the elementary and high schools, teachers have been trained to follow curricula organized around textbooks. Complete with built in course outlines, pretested reading levels, teachers'

TABLE XI-2: Education Market Sales as Percentage of Total Publisher Receipts for General Books

	1976
Trade	30.6
Adult hardbound	23.1
Adult paperbound	34.6
Juvenile	25.1
Religious	12.1
Professional	23.4
Mass market paperbacks	17.5
University press	38.5
Book clubs and mail order	12.4
Total	19.9

SOURCE: Knowledge Industry Publications, Inc. from AAP *Industry Statistics, 1976.*

guidebooks and sometimes suggested examinations, the textbooks are designed as teaching materials. Trade books, as applicable as they may be for any course, nonetheless require extra work by the teacher to be integrated into a course. In higher education, instructors in many disciplines are used to putting together their own reading lists from source materials, but even here areas such as the sciences and business still depend largely on texts.

Therefore, to expand their forays into this field, publishers must not only make their lists known to teachers and those in charge of title decisions but they must structure their titles beforehand to fit into standard course areas. And if they are really serious about selling to the school markets, they should be active in educating the educators on how to teach using their materials.

Most trade and mass market paperback houses that expect to make education sales a significant part of their business have created separate education divisions — not textbook divisions, but editorial and marketing groups that can concentrate on repackaging consumer titles and selling them to the schools. Obviously, there is a cost involved. But given the fact that sales are all of books that have already been justified and created for the consumer/library market, the rewards to the publisher could prove substantial.

TABLE XI-3: Education Attainment, Adult Population,[1] Selected Years, 1940-1976

	Percent completing 4 years of High School or more	Percent who have 4 or more years of College	Median Year Completed
1940	24.5%	4.6%	8.6
1950	34.3	6.2	9.3
1960	41.1	7.7	10.5
1970	55.2	11.0	12.2
1973	59.8	12.6	12.3
1976	64.1	14.7	12.4

[1] 25 years and older.

SOURCE: U.S. Bureau of Census: U.S. Census of Population and Current Population Reports, series P-20 and unpublished data.

There are several alternative channels for marketing to the schools that parallel those for the consumer/library market: direct from trade and paperback publishers, through national or regional jobbers, via local IDs, and by special classroom book clubs.

Motivated publishers have combed their backlists for books

that may be suitable for packaging into curriculum units. The Random House Reading Program is a case in point. Each unit includes as many as 50 trade titles, each with its own added student learning materials and teacher guide. To do this, Random House employed professionals to perform reading difficulty analyses for each book, resulting in packages that contain material both several levels below and several above the designated recommended grade level on the package. The units were eventually expanded to include records and sound filmstrips.

Bantam, Dell, and, more recently, Avon are among the paperback houses that are active in the education market. The mass market publishers have an affinity for creating special imprints for their school book lines, using more low-keyed covers, sometimes better paper, and supporting materials. Educators have long been somewhat skeptical of the use of paperbacks in the classroom, despite the acknowledged quality of the scholarly Mentor line developed by New American Library as early as 1948. But college instructors were the first to accept the quality paperbacks, such as Doubleday's Anchor Books, and these led to quick acceptance of the mass market books. Most of the first reprints were of classics, both old and more modern, as evidenced by such imprints as Bantam Classics or Signet Classics. Beginning in 1963, Bantam put out a separate, distinctly packaged and recognizable line for high school students, the Pathfinder Editions. These included a reading level index as a teacher aid. Its impact was farreaching: John Steinbeck's *The Pearl*, which had already sold a million copies for adults, sold more than 4 million copies in the next six years as a Pathfinder. Dell uses its Laurel line for college level reprints and originals, Delta for higher-priced, larger size books. Avon has introduced several juvenile imprints for these markets.

Bantam, a pioneer in reaching the school markets, not only has prepared course plans for a staggering variety of subjects but is not too proud to draw from other hardcover and paperback lists when appropriate to supplement its own collection. Its course planning guides for teachers outline step by step how each course can be scheduled and presented.

Getting paperbacks distributed

Compared to the trade houses, paperback publishers are at even a greater disadvantage in selling to the education market, especially below the college level. Trade houses have long depended on the library market and library jobbers for a substantial portion of their sales. Mass market paperback publishers have been more retail oriented, looking to the IDs for the bulk of their distribution. Although this works relatively well in getting paperbacks to newsstands and drugstores, the wholesalers are least equipped to sell to the education market. At most, 15 wholesalers have made major efforts in this regard, despite recognition by the Council for Periodical Distributors Association of the importance of the education market. The Magazine and Paperback Marketing Institute publishes a weighy tome called *The MPMI Educational Sales Manual,*" giving IDs step by step instructions for soliciting educational sales, but evidently few have the inclination or resources to mine this lode.

In contrast with schools, selling to the higher education market is relatively easy. Most sales at the college and university level are made through the campus bookstores. The bulk of these sales are for books ordered by instructors as required reading for their courses, especially in the social sciences and humanities. Although some trade houses employ representatives who call on college faculty rather than retailers, the predominant way of reaching faculty is through catalogues. Again, the paperback houses have been active in this regard, putting out special catalogues specifically designed for college faculty. Books are listed by subject matter, such as American literature, communications and media, and psychology. These catalogues must include information regarding procedures for acquiring examination copies and the conditions under which free desk copies will be made available to faculty.

Most books assigned for courses are ordered through the school bookstores, just as textbooks. Ideally, these books are chosen months in advance so delivery should not prove a problem, with most popular titles available from the National Association of

College Stores' own distribution center. And, in theory at least, publishers should find themselves with few returns. Unfortunately, such are not always the ways of academia. Frequently book decisions are made late. Course enrollments too often grossly exceed, or fall short of, expectations. Then, some students do not buy all the assigned readings, choosing to share with another, get the book from a library, or, in the case of hardbacks, buy a used edition. Publishers have rebelled at taking back large numbers of unbought books and many set limits on the percentage of the original order they will accept as returns.

Sales specialists and jobbers

To reach the school markets, Bantam uses education sales specialists, meeting with principals, teachers, and boards of education. Most publishers attend some of the many education conferences and conventions, but the effectiveness of attendance at these sessions, balanced against the cost, is being increasingly questioned. Besides the usual catalogues and book fairs, Avon has relied heavily on education jobbers who understand the school market. Avon is also using cassettes and audiovisual aids to promote its books. The AAP is helping "educate the educators" in the use of general books through in-service days in suburban areas, so far restricted to the East.

Jobbers and wholesalers, who have viewed themselves heretofore as merely order takers and distributors, have become more aggressive in their role as a sales force. The nation's largest, Baker & Taylor, though primarily a library jobber of trade books, has backed into the education market through its entry into the sale of audiovisual media beginning in 1972. But once having set up a separate sales force to sell (rather than just take orders), the company decided to add trade books, which, in turn, required B&T to expand its inventory to include the popular paperback format. B&T is now involved in putting together its own packages, including combined record or audio cassette and book units.

Baker & Taylor doubled the size of its sales force of 50, having found that the place to sell now is in the school *building* – to teachers and department heads. Jobbers, unlike the publishers, can be active in *assembling* products and marketing them, backed by their already existing inventory and distribution networks.

STUDENT BOOK CLUBS

One of the most well-established approaches to bringing books into the schools is through the paperback book clubs run by Scholastic Magazines, Inc., the ground breaker, as well as My Weekly Reader Book Clubs (run by Xerox Education Publications), Reader's Digest programs, and the Young Readers Club of Pocket Books. Scholastic Magazines alone was responsible for the distribution of some 55 million paperback books to el-hi classrooms during the 1974-75 academic year. Half of the country's high schools and almost 75% of the elementary schools have a Scholastic book club.

One of the major challenges of these clubs is finding enough appropriate editorial material for the students. The other difficulty is the economic realities of having to fulfill classroom orders of one or two copies of many titles of low cost books (the top price rarely exceeds $1.25, the average is close to $.60 or $.70). There is some concern among publishers exploring the education markets as to just how elastic prices are on paperbacks — the feeling being that there may be more price resistance than for adult paperbacks.

Scholastic has five clubs, each for a different grade level, but spanning the entire K-12 range. Similar to their adult club counterparts, the school clubs offer 10 to 15 new titles each month. Promotion is through direct mailings to teachers, as well as exhibits at the educators' conferences and, at least in Scholastic's case, a field sales force. For their help, teachers get a free book for every five ordered. But despite the excitement generated by the book clubs in many classrooms, Scholastic and the other clubs leave it up to the teachers to decide how to use the books for classroom exercises. The clubs foster an interest in paperbacks at an early age and draw on that interest through school, further adding to their acceptability. As a result, many students now eschew hardbacks in favor of a paper version because they are used to the feel and convenient size.

THE MATURING OF THE EDUCATION MARKET

Although trade and mass market paperback publishers have a substantial stake and interest in the education markets, there are still obstacles to be overcome. At the el-hi level, both trade and paperback houses must learn how to sell to the schools, meaning putting together a useful package and then knowing how to market it. The early emphasis was in the higher education market, with Bantam taking a lead in reaching out for the el-hi population. But even Bantam is a relative novice in this field, whereas Avon has barely gotten past square one. The trade houses have been reaping the rewards of the university expansion, but that big push is over now and they will have to turn in the el-hi direction themselves for new opportunities. Publishers with both trade and text divisions have a decided advantage in this regard, if they can get coordinated enough to exploit it.

The trade and mass market publishers have been hitting their heads against a stone wall in getting college bookstores to expand their general book departments. According to AAP calculations, 1000 college bookstores (out of 2200 members of the National Association of College Stores) should carry trade books and do not. Only 300 have first-rate general book departments. Currently college stores are selling about $120 million (at retail level) of nonrequired general books, compared to over $500 million in new course books and another $45 million in used books. Although general books have an average gross margin for the college stores of 29%, versus only 20% for textbooks, student supplies average 37% and other merchandise 31%. With an ever growing profit-consciousness at the college store, managers have less interest in the hassles of running a good book department.

Nonetheless, the outlook, both short and long run, is encouraging for general book publishers. Even if the "back to basics" movement in school districts has a depressing effect on sums allocated for films and AV media, it should not hurt books. In the long run, the tight, lock-step curriculum of old is not going to return, giving teachers more freedom to create and experiment with individualized instruction and courses. For these, paperbacks, both mass market and trade, are ideally suited. They are less expensive than hardbacks and more adaptable.

Moreover, the paperback has finally come of age, having overcome considerable professional resistance. Today many librarians report that their paperback collections are the most popular materials in the library. Mass market publishers can now include school sales in their projection of total sales. The books that paperback houses sell best in the schools are not the best selling adult authors, but quality backlist books.

The rise in prominence of the schools as a market is already having a bearing on what gets published in paperback. What else would explain Bantam's decision to publish a new translation of *The Aeneid*, hardly a mass market bestseller. At the same time, the school book clubs have found such a dearth of appropriate material to reprint that they are commissioning a greater number of original titles specifically for their clubs. Although fiction is the overwhelming favorite for the el-hi crowd's pleasure reading (just the opposite of adult trends), overall, the school market continues to be dominated by nonfiction titles.

The hardback trade houses that have juvenile lines are also encouraged, despite annual figures and population trends that show a declining curve in this field. As prominent a house as William Morrow is adding significantly to its juvenile trade list.

Paperback houses, however, must be particularly concerned with their image to get their foot into the schoolhouse door. Avon has been working hard at this and finds that the strategy pays off: its school and college sales have "zoomed" since it has begun concentrating on titles that are believed appropriate for this market.

Even with a leveling off of enrollments and a less rapid growth of funding, the school and college market, especially the former, remains a frontier for general book publishers, one that those with the best backlists and marketing organizations will find lucrative.

XII

Expanding Outlets and Formats

Every distribution channel or form of selling of books was at one time new, experimental, or "revolutionary," such as the innovative book clubs of the 1920s or the paperback format of the 1940s. Today these have been integrated into the industry as normal and accepted facets of book publishing and marketing. There are a number of similar concepts in the early stages of development today that have the potential to both modify and expand the base and nature of book publishing over the next decade.

DISTRIBUTION

The international market

U.S. exports of domestically produced books soared during the 1960s and have resumed a healthy growth after a brief slowdown at the start of the 1970s. The total expansion from 1960 through 1976 of 483% in current dollars (Table XII-1) exceeds the rate of growth of total U.S. exports of all merchandise of 457% for that period. Nearly half of the book exports were to one country, Canada. These figures do not include revenues from books published by foreign subsidiaries of U.S. based companies. There has been little attention to this market by the mass market paperback publishers, who shipped a total of 12 million books to foreign markets in 1972 (the last year for which unit figures are available) out of a total volume of 141 million units, or 8.5%.

To be sure, there are some massive problems to be overcome in developing overseas markets: 1) There is only a limited audience for the English-language versions, especially in the developing countries. 2) Various national egos must not be bruised by heavy-handed intrusions of foreign books. The feeling is that sales of these books may lessen the demand for books by native authors. 3) It takes close cooperation and coordination to be able to judge which books are properly suited for a given nation.

Nonetheless, certain publishers do see a bright future in foreign markets, relying on translated versions, and co-publishing arrangements with their own subsidiaries or independent foreign houses. Subscription reference book publishers, for example, have been placing increasing emphasis on their overseas sales of English language as well as translated versions of the American sets, to the point where an estimated 47% of encyclopedia revenues of American publishers are accounted for through international sales. Reader's Digest has long been mining the foreign markets with translations, whereas Time-Life Books has had some series translated into as many as 26 languages. Time-Life claims that its foreign sales are expanding more rapidly than its domestic volume, using offices in Amsterdam, London, Paris, and Mexico City to handle co-publishing or consortium printing arrangements (in which expensive four-color printing is done at one time, with the texts in various languages being added separately). Time-Life in its

TABLE XII-1:   U.S. Book Exports[1]

	Value of Shipments (millions)	Average Annual % Change
1960	$ 51.2	–
1965	99.9	19.0%
1970	171.7	14.4
1973	194.5	4.4
1976	298.3	17.8
Compounded annual increase 1960-1976		11.6%

[1] Value of shipments over $250. The actual total is estimated at an additional 50%.

SOURCE: U.S. Department of Commerce, *Bureau of the Census,* FT-410.

foreign sales depends primarily on the same direct mail approach used at home, with adaptations as needed. In Latin America, in one instance, the poor postal system has forced Time-Life to rely on door-to-door sales. McGraw-Hill has a sales force at work in 82 countries.

Leasing of foreign rights to American books has been an alternative to publishing or exporting overseas. Both translation rights and English language reprint rights are available for licensing arrangements, subject to provisions of the Universal Copyright Convention. A 1974 antitrust suit against 21 U.S. publishers by the Justice Department alleged a conspiracy among the publishers and the British Publishers Association "to divide the world market into exclusive territories and to allocate the exclusive territories among themselves." At issue is the right of authors to assign copyright. A consent decree entered into by the parties in 1976 bars American publishers from entering into licensing arrangements for exclusive territorial grants and effectively puts responsibility for deciding on the best approach to foreign markets on the individual publisher. The results should include a diminishing of licensing rights to British markets and greater American exports.

Of course, the international market for books is a two-way street. U.S. book imports have been rising as rapidly as exports, and large foreign publishers are increasingly establishing beachheads here. Just in the period 1973 to 1977, Collins & Sons acquired World Publishing; Istituto Finanziaro Industriale, the Agnelli family conglomerate, bought Bantam Books and sold a majority interest to Germany's Bertelsmann; Elsevier Publishing Co., a Dutch giant, purchased Dutton; International Publishing Co., another British firm, absorbed A&W; Penguin Books, part of the Pearson Longman publishing group, took over Viking Press; Morgan Grampian bought David McKay, and Thomson of Great Britain acquired Wadsworth.

Nonbookstore outlets — the special interest market

Special interest books — like their magazine cousins — appeal to participant/activists in a given field. Books on gardening, hobbies, home or auto repairs, and other how-to books including cookbooks, are designed for people who expect to engage in the activity they describe. Often these people are not otherwise book buyers. But they are perfect customers for information media relating to their interests. Publishers with strong backlists in these fields are finding that, rather than expecting the doers to come to them, via a bookstore, they must seek out customers in other outlets. In such instances, the book market becomes secondary to the special interest market. Many people who do not read for pleasure will buy a book that is germane to a special interest – if the book is readily accessible to them. This means that publishers must initiate the search for nontraditional retail outlets for their materials.

Even with the expansion in the number of bookstores, the access of much of the population to books is still quite limited. Although mail order and book clubs are one response to this problem, they still have their limitations of reach, economics, and selection. Along with Chilton Books, Crown Publishers has been making a concerted effort to sell books in nontraditional outlets. The key, explains Crown's Mike Friedman, is to pinpoint a specific market and sell constantly to this group. "Some people are intimidated by books and just won't walk into a bookstore," Friedman theorizes. The response is to make books available where they do go.

As one notably successful case, Crown has worked at getting its arts and crafts series books sold in hobby shops, though it is not as easily said as done. To sell to the nonbook trade, publishers must research and work through the distribution channels of the trade they are trying to reach. They must adapt to its discount structure and trade policies. Failure to do so will result in a rejection by the outside industry. In the hobby business, Crown found that even if its displays at the hobby industry association conventions aroused dealer interest, it could not depend on the retailers to place orders through book wholesalers. Moreover, hobby dealers were not particularly pleased with the lower than their normal discounts offered for books. Crown also discovered that wholesalers in the hobby business were specialists in leather, or beads, or stained glass, etc., rather than general arts and crafts wholesalers. As a result of research, as well as much trial and error, Crown made contacts to distribute through that industry's whole-salers, offering its books at higher than usual discounts, but requiring larger orders and with a no return proviso (which is standard for other goods in the hobby business anyway). Crown advertises through hobby industry trade publications and has uncovered a large mail order business as well.

Selling crafts books in hobby stores to a built-in clientele of hobbyists makes sense. The same is true of gardening books in plant stores or camera books in photography shops. Ideas for new topics in these fields can be appropriately bounced off the target trade, rather than within the book community. The idea is to sell the product not as a book, but as an extension of the tools and equipment of the particular subject matter. Museum bookshops have been doing this for years. At the International Center for Photography, a small New York museum for contemporary photography, the small 185-title bookshop sells one or more books, ranging in price from $3.95 to $40 to over 10% of those who come through the facility.

One of the publishers that has been most successful at selling books in hobby outlets is Lane Magazine & Book Co., publisher of the Sunset Books line of cooking, travel, and how-to books. With its carefully controlled list (constantly pruned and updated), a standard size and format, plus special racks and other merchandising aids, Lane has greatly expanded nationwide distribution over the last six years, starting from its base as a regional California publisher. It now sells 10 million books a year, a sizable proportion of these (though less than half) in nonbook outlets such as hardware and gardening supply stores.

Bulk sales for premiums

Crown has also been aggressive in pursuing the premium business, marketing its trade titles to banks, trade associations, and consumer goods manufacturers for them to sell or give away to customers. One effort enabled Crown to sell an Italian cookbook on its list to Ronzoni, the pasta company. Ronzoni then offered the book for $1 plus a boxtop, resulting in sales of over 300,000 copies over the years. Banks use books as an incentive to open an account, newspapers or magazines use books as renewal incentives. A billiards book was sold under a special arrangement with Brunswick. Often the publisher actually handles the fulfillment.

Putting together these deals does involve much work and is a high risk undertaking: negotiations may take a year. In most cases, the publisher must engage in a hard sell, convincing the buyer that the premium will be self-liquidating or will result in increased business. Crown exhibits at premium shows, but also engages in direct mailings of special interest books to association leaders or jobbers in that field.

The Benjaman Co. in New York specializes in creating paperback books as premiums, and a number of the mass market paperback houses have plumbed this market on their own.

NEW FORMATS

Large format paperbound

Trade publishers have been involved in paperbound editions for many years. These have differed from the mass market paperbound books in three ways: 1) they are distributed primarily through trade channels; 2) they cover a much wider range of topics including works of philosophy, history, or literary craticism that rarely find their way into mass market lists; 3) they are usually, but not invariably, of a larger size than the standard rack size mass market paperback.

Mass market houses have of late blurred this last distinction, having found that with certain topics they too could sell larger sized paperbound books through their usual channels at a higher price than they have been accustomed to. Examples include Avon's *Best of Life* at $7.95, New American Library/Harry Abrams *Art of Walt Disney* at the same price, and Bantam's edition of William Manchester's *The Glory and the Dream* priced at $6.95

Large format paperbacks have been both originals and reprints: both "Life" and "Disney" came from hardcover, but *The Last Whole Earth Catalog* was a successful original. Certain types of editorial matter are most appropriate for this larger size, particularly subjects requiring artwork. Those publishers in the field believe that the large formats are the beginning of a great phenomenon for the industry, arguing that:

• They create a new market for books. Movers behind Book-of-the-Month Club's Quality Paperback Service are convinced that there is a separate audience for the lower priced trade paperback editions. Avon echoed this sentiment. With its reprint of *Watership Down* already a mass market bestseller, Avon came out with a trade paperback edition of the book, confident that it would find a separate niche. To bolster this line of reasoning, former Avon editor in chief Peter Mayer cited the simultaneous publishing of a cloth and trade paper edition of the *New York Times Cookbook* with sales of both doing well. American West Publishing Co. has recently begun producing quality paperbound editions of its lavishly illustrated books, believing that the editions will be displayed in a separate section of the bookstore and won't hurt hardcover sales.

• As a corollary to the first point, the large size paperbacks, with their superior printing, paper, and binding, have opened up paperbacks to the gift market. At a $7.95 price tag, the value is more apparent. Using shrink wrapping to keep them fresh, the reprint art books can themselves find their way to coffee tables.

• The higher unit sale of the trade or large sized paperbacks means more dollars at each level. Whereas the sale of more than 100,000 copies of a hardback book is a rare occurrence, more trade paperbacks reach this level, and in the case of books such as *Joy of Sex* or *Best of Life*, at prices approaching hardcover prices.

There are some clouds in Eden, needless to say. The key to successful large format size is still quality, such as the innovative *Whole Earth Catalog*. For retailers, the larger, more expensive paperbacks will put a burden on their inventory, since they do not turn over as fast as the mass market paperbacks. Moreover, the art books are easily dogeared and damaged from browsing, making returns less certain. Even if shrink wrapped, at least one copy will have to be sacrificed for thumbing through. The large books also put a strain on display space, since they do not fit into common racks and must be given high visibility. Another problem facing both booksellers and publishers is the need to educate customers. Richard Hinman, of the Harvard Co-operative Society, reported a certain resistance on the part of browsers, who are not used to paying $8.95 for a paperback book.

The irony of the pricing is that the manufacturing cost of a large-size paperback is virtually the same as a clothbound book of equal quality and print run. The only difference is the $.50 or so material cost for the boards that go into the hardbound version. The economics of the paperback variety require high print orders to get good quality at a low price.

All these reasons are enough for some publishers to stand clear of the rush to do large format paperbacks. Says one savvy publisher with experience in hardcover, trade paperback, and mass market fields: "There's no way to publish trade paperbacks with the kind of advances that mass market paperback houses are used to paying, and still make money."

Nonetheless, the large format paperbacks, coming now from mass market publishers as well as the traditional trade houses, promise to add another alternative to printing format decisions, as well as new avenues for marketing. Although they may inject more confusion into the battle for rights to print a given work in each format, they promise also to open up new markets for books, while further blurring the sanctity of the channels of distribution. Trade paperback publishers, who at one time sold almost exclusively to the college market, now find that they can publish more for general audiences, distributing to bookstores and better mass market outlets as well; mass market publishers can invade the serious bookstores with the higher-priced books, yet maintain their base of traditional outlets.

Hardcover reprints

An outgrowth of the boom in remaindering (Chapter IX) has been a surge in the business of reprinting certain hardcover books for sale in the remainder style. One problem with the remainder business has been the limited number of good products available. Once a particular lot was sold, there was no more. Yet booksellers and some remainder outfits found that expensive art or picture books that did not sell well at $20 almost walked away for $8. To meet this demand for expensive looking sales merchandise, Crown Publishers instituted a new imprint, Bonanza, which buys the rights to a successful remainder book from the original publisher, paying royalties on sales. (Publishers do not pay royalties to authors on copies of the overstocks they remainder.) Crown, or other publishers in this field, then print large quantities of the book from the original plates, usually on paper stock comparable to the original, or somewhat lower in quality. Incurring no editorial development cost nor prepress costs, while printing in large quantities, Bonanza books can be priced in line with the distressed priced remainders. Crown aggressively prices many of these books at three times manufacturing cost, vs. the traditional hardcover formula of 6-7 times. On occasion, the original publisher will tack on additional copies to the print run, so that the publisher may continue to sell these in small quantities at the higher price (yet at the lower costs which come from a high-volume run). This also helps promote the bargain image of the reprints with a "selling elsewhere at $40" type promotion.

For the most part, the prestige publishers are more comfortable with the Bonanza arrangement than printing high volume, low cost editions themselves in order not to lessen their image and reduce their ability to sell future high price editions of other books. These reprint editions, by the way, are not listed on their own in Bowker's *Books in Print*. There are bookstores, such as the Marboro chain, which handle almost nothing but remainders and reprints, doing a large volume of mail order as well as retail trade. Crown does its own mail order selling through catalogues bearing the Outlet Book Co. name.

The remainder/reprint business actually dates back to reprints of titles by their original publisher under different imprints, but this was discontinued before World War II. For almost twenty years after the war, Outlet Book Co. was the only one to engage in reprints (other than the small edition scholarly reprints by small houses such as Arno Press). However, the $25 million remainder business now has encouraged the entry of new firms, including A&W Promotional Books, Harlem Book Co., and Walden Book Co.'s resale division.

The typical reprint is designed to sell at about half the cost of the original retail edition. This is possible for the reasons stated previously, as well as the greater predictability of the quantities needed, since there is now a sales history for the book. Moreover, only books that have sold well as remainders are reprinted. Unlike original publishers, who are new product developers, the reprinters consider themselves repackagers and marketers, establishing a fundamental difference in outlook between the two. The reprinters can choose from what is available, picking the best titles of several publishers to sell as a package. They can then offer to retailers in a single catalogue or showroom an entire, integrated line of subjects and prices.

In providing this wide range of product to the bookseller, the reprint/remainder publisher is also functioning as a jobber, simplifying the work of the book retailer. This relatively new marketing device is also being used as a means to try some basic changes in the discount and return structure. Unlike most trade billing, the reprinters are offering cash discounts with ten day EOM terms, in effect offering an extra 1%-2% discount to all customers. In addition, Walden gives an option of a 50% no returns discount. The bargain-price aspect of reprints and remainders makes them ideal traffic builders for stores that are predominantly nonbook merchandisers, like department stores and discounters, further broadening the market.

There are many similarities between the hardcover reprinters today and the mass market paperback industry several decades ago. Both industries deal in merchandise originally produced by other publishers and both have developed channels of distribution and marketing methods other than those used by traditional trade publishers. There are a limited number of companies in both fields, limiting the amount of communication circuits necessary to maintain contact between retailers and suppliers. There are differences, for sure, particularly in the type of books each handles; the hardcover reprinters are mostly interested in special interest nonfiction and art books, generally ignoring fiction.

But both have provided products that broaden the market for books. The remainder and reprint channels have brought to the attention of a much greater public many titles that on their original publication are lost in the forest of competing books. Such books are often overpriced for their intended audience. Their success at much lower prices is evidence that there is a clientele out there for books, provided they are more thoughtfully and forcefully marketed.

PRINTING ON DEMAND

In the textbook field, several small operations are now providing a service that permits an instructor to order a custom-made text, combining articles, materials from other textbooks, and even original materials. The originals are copied and printed offset and clipped into binders.

A much more futurist vision has been explored by Xerox. A scenario, 1985: A student wants a book, written about 12 years earlier. It is about a shark that attacks some bathers and a teacher suggested that it would be good book to read for an American literature course. The library's copy has been missing for years. The bookstore is rather small, perhaps 800 square feet, but from past experience, you know that it contains most of the 625,000 titles "in print." The proprietor checks a microform file for the book, *Jaws*, and proceeds to a bank of file cabinets, from which he takes a roll of film and places it in a machine. He punches the International Standard Book Number for *Jaws* into a keyboard and within seconds, pages start zipping out of the machine. In less than a minute, the entire book has been printed and a separate device quickly binds the pages and wraps a cardboard cover around. The cost is $9.00 (1977 dollars) and time elapsed five minutes.

The technology to print on demand from a microfilm master is here today, though the speed and economics are not yet available. But Xerox is reported to have conducted a study of the book publishing, manufacturing, and distribution network to help evaluate the feasibility of printing on demand. Its conclusion appears to have been to let the idea simmer on the back burner. The concept, however, is impressive. This isn't a Buck Rogers plan for computer storage of all the works of man, with highspeed print out at the touch of a few keys. That too can be done but even at today's dramatically lowered cost of storage, it simply does not look financially feasible. More promising is the reduction of all but the most current bestsellers into microform, with high-speed photocopying machines to reproduce a given title when requested. A bookstore would have a hardcopy of the most frequently requested titles (generated from the microform) on display in the store. Mass market paperback versions of current fast-moving titles would be printed as at present, but once the demand slowed down, they would be printed only on demand.

Of course, the widespread and inexpensive application of copying procedures has resulted in much consternation and legal battles between publishers and libraries over the extent to which copying from copyrighted books and magazines can be done without paying royalties. Before publishers are willing to license either booksellers or libraries to print their books on demand, they will insist on careful safeguards, including an accounting system, to ensure that they are compensated for each copy that is made.

Such a method of printing would dramatically change the nature of book production and distribution — eliminating a large part of the function performed by commercial printers, and slashing the high cost of moving millions of books around the country. But since these costs are only 10%-15% of the retail price of a book, they would not automatically lead to steep reductions in selling price. Nor would application of this technology reduce the need for market research, advertising, promotion, and other activities. Indeed, the lower entry costs might encourage a magnified outpouring of titles, making it even harder and more costly to bring a book to the attention of prospective customers. The technology of on-demand printing would be most valuable for specialized and scholarly works that go to a strictly limited audience, and for which a significant reduction in make-ready and plant costs can spell the difference between publishing and not publishing.

XIII

Summary and Conclusions

There is something about the book business that sets it spiritually apart from the multitude of other industries and trades. It is the charm and the attraction of working in the field despite its low salaries and profit margins. But it is simultaneously the frustration of coping with a business where 30,000 new products are added to 475,000 old ones in a single year. It is the literary quality of the trade editors, but it extends to the gait of the salesman on the road. At the American Booksellers Association annual trade show, it is the 8000 or 9000 booksellers from around the country crowding the publishers' displays, anxious to pick up, flip through the pages of the latest works. It is a small circle of executives who know each other well and move from one house to another, but always keeping their hand in the trade. Finally, it is the sentiment of publishers sniffing at competitors who call their books "products."

But this feel or rhythm of the book industry is a musty sensation. Increasingly, others in the industry are insisting that what they sell *is* a product and should be treated as such. These are the managers who have come to book publishing or selling from electronics companies, the retail trade, or home products industries. They have no commitment to books *per se*, but they do see an opportunity for profit by making the publishing and sale of books more successful. These are the executives of the burgeoning retail chains, the promoters of the hardcover reprints, the publishers of the bus station paperbacks, and the wholesale jobbers taking their cut from both ends. Many of the traditionalists in the industry disdain them, as much for their motives as for their actions.

A third group tries to steer a middle course. These are the publishers who, though they understand that books are a product and must be marketed as such, also know that books have an image, an intangible scent of importance. Their task, and the real challenge for the book publishing industry, is to maintain this feel among the current hard core of book buyers, the readers of the *New Yorker* for want of a better image, while at the same time bringing into the fold the tens of millions of people who look now to the television or other media for spending their leisure time, and who are book buyers only on rare occasions, such as selecting a gift or picking up a paperback blockbuster like *The Godfather* or *The Exorcist.*

NEW MARKETS

There remains a vast untapped market for general books. There is still room for inroads in the educational area, especially in certain curricula such as adult continuing education. Paperback books of all kinds have considerable opportunity to explore the el-hi market. Another promising barely tapped market consists of the imaginative use of nontraditional outlets, such as health food or hobby stores for books concerning those subjects. Making books available where they have not been before, such as the Family Reading Centers in supermarkets or the book departments that are appearing with ever increasing frequency in the national retail chains such as Penney's and Sears, brings masses of people into contact with the publishers' products.

DISTRIBUTION

The key to an orderly distribution system must be the strengthening of the currently weak network of intermediaries: the wholesalers and jobbers who service the retail trade. In selling to library customers, jobber specialists are already the predominant factor, plainly because publishers cannot accept handling so many orders for small quantities of books, whereas libraries do not have the human resources to deal with all the publishers. On the other hand, booksellers have enjoyed dealing directly with the publishers — part of the mystique of the trade, despite the complexities and inefficiences of doing so. Moreover, by never establishing a separate discount structure for wholesalers, publishers made it difficult for them to carve out their niche.

Through no strategy of the AAP or ABA, there is now developing a national jobber network that may lead the way in the change. In adapting a minimal technology of inventory control and reporting, Ingram Book Co. (and others who have followed) has created a service that makes dealing with the wholesaler more overtly profitable, despite the lower gross margin. If Ingram succeeds in establishing regional warehouses that are reasonably well stocked, the industry finally may have run out of reasons to promote direct retailer/publisher dealings for all but the largest booksellers.

To a great extent, the ability of the jobbers to function on a widespread scale will depend on the decisions of the publishers themselves. Bantam, for one, has long encouraged a bookstore or school customer to work through the local wholesalers or jobbers, though of course it cannot turn down an order from someone who insists. But if publishers wish to shed their cumbersome and slow order fulfillment operations, they must not only send the small customer to the wholesalers but many of the larger ones as well — no middlemen can perform well if they get just the castoffs.

The ABA has a major role to play in this regard. Up to now it has promoted the idea of direct ordering from the publisher, regarding jobbers as an emergency "fill in stock" stopgap. One of the ABA's high priority tasks should be the initiation of an information-gathering project to analyze carefully the true cost to bookselling operations of varying sizes of having to deal directly through the publisher, contrasting the 2%-3% extra discount percentages with the direct cost of such practices. The booksellers at this point must be educated and it is the strong conclusion of this study that with a comprehensive canvassing of members' cost structures, the ABA will come up with a recommendation favoring dealing with jobbers on a larger scale than currently for most retailers.

In fact, the future direction of the distribution channels for general books may be more in the hands of the booksellers than the publishers. The publishers are most interested in maintaining the closest control possible over their product. Just as they want to find and develop manuscripts, they also want to distribute and promote their own titles. Even should analysis show a cash savings in using jobbers to a greater extent, they may still feel that the greater control they maintain in being able to sell directly to retailers offsets this savings. However, should bookstore owners insist that they would rather work through intermediaries, for the reasons already enumerated, then publishers would, of course, have to go along. It can be the example of Sessler's in Philadelphia, which almost overnight increased its buying from a jobber 150% when an adequate mechanism was presented, that will lead the publishers down the path to greater efficiency despite themselves.

Where does this leave publishers' representatives and commission salesmen? They can still perform their roles of informing booksellers of titles in the lines they represent, but in the end, the orders they write will be fulfilled through the jobber of the retailer's choice. Thus, a bookseller that deals with Ingram will have all the publishers' reps forward orders for the new books and backlist titles to that jobber. Ingram could then send the bookseller all the ordered books from the various publishers in two or three shipments (as they become available to the jobber), instead of several dozen publishers each fulfilling a separate order. Orders so received by the jobbers will require a commission back to the publisher, whereas orders received directly from the bookseller will be handled as they are now.

Such a system will also encourage the jobbers to stock a wider variety of books, since they would want to carry most of the titles for which the publishers' reps are getting orders. Mass market paperbacks can be similarly handled, with the independent distributors continuing to service their magazine accounts. Still, many titles are too infrequently ordered to be carried by the regular jobbers and must be special ordered. Two solutions appear feasible. One is for a major library jobber, such as Baker & Taylor, which already carries huge inventories, to modify its systems to be able to readily and profitably handle these requests. The other is for a Bookamatic-type operation to try again, only this time setting up shop only when and if enough publishers will agree on the procedures and financial arrangements.

TOO MANY TITLES?

A frequent complaint within the industry is that there are simply too many new titles being issued — implying that publishers are not discriminating enough in what they send to the market. Although there certainly had been a steady escalation in the number of new titles until 1975, this was an overblown excuse for the other failings of the marketing mechanisms of the industry for several reasons. First, the number of new titles and editions issued annually between 1965 and 1974 increased 43%, but in the same period book sales increased by 53%.

Second, the most rapidly growing area of new titles is in books that are largely designated for the education market, whether textbooks or allied books, a situation that has little in common with the dilemma of marketing trade and general books. For example, looking at Table II-10, fully one-sixth of all the new titles issued in 1976 were in the sociology and economics disciplines, compared to barely 10% that are categorized as "fiction."

Third, highly specialized professional books — law, medicine, business, science and technology — represented 20% of the new editions and titles in 1976. Many of these books are also designed for the education market, but they are successfully sold in small quantities through highly effective mail order operations as well, since the markets for these special interest subjects are tightly defined and accessible through mailing lists.

Finally, industry-wide solutions to the "problem" of too many titles are impossible anyway. Certainly no agreement among publishers can be proposed to limit the number of new titles that will be published. The go/no-go decision for publishing each new title is one that each house must make based on its own evaluation of its ability to handle the publication, and its feeling for the need of such a title. Whereas prudent business sense might be encouraged, such as some amount of market research or sundry financial considerations, the decision to publish or not to publish a new title must be made from the point of view of each publisher and not on what some amorphous "industry" considers beneficial. After all, book publishing is reasonably close to a free market, and publishers that overproduce will pay the penalty in diminished profits or even losses. This economic reality, rather than a resort to consortia for managing output, is the best guarantee against overproduction. This has apparently been the case, as new titles have declined in 1975 and 1976.

A wide range of titles is a healthy sign of diversity in thought. It gives the potential buyer alternatives in many subject areas and replaces out-of-date books with a stream of fresh information. Indeed, the demands placed on the distribution system by such a wealth of books are substantial, but in truth it must be vigorously argued that the responsibility of the publishing and retailing industry is to hone a network that will cope efficiently with the sum of this knowledge and entertainment. To propose that it be limited is to starve the patient in order to save it.

RETAIL BOOKSELLING

The growth of the Waldens and Daltons and Paperback Booksmiths is an encouraging sign for this side of the business. These serve as hard proof to the doubters that retail bookselling can be profitable and provide a return on investment that is commensurate with other forms of retailing. Although their individual and combined buying clout may give some cause for concern, this apprehension is misdirected. By reacting favorably toward an editorial idea — or in suggesting one themselves based on widespread feedback from customers — the chains can be a positive force in creating new books, while giving publishers an added degree of stability in their print order plans. It is not likely, however, that a good manuscript which would have been published before the chains existed would not now see print, even if the chain buyers were not excited about it. The chain stores should signal independent booksellers that the time is here for their own expansion.

Another promising development has been the interest of the national chain department stores in adding book centers to their operations. The old method of having several racks of books serviced by local independent distributors in each territory was too unsystematic, hardly in keeping with the merchandising flair of the chains. Now, with the aggressive marketing of Charles Levy Co.'s Computer Book Service, the Penney's, Kresge's, and Sears' are finding a workable way to include full-fledged book departments in their stores, with the selection of books customized to the sales pattern of each separate location. If more of the larger independent distributors develop basic information systems for their major customers, the already successful Family Reading Center concept would be that much more salable and would result in greater turnover for everyone involved. In this last regard, however, it is crucial that paperback booksellers in particular resign themselves to the inclusion of Universal Product Code markings on their book covers.

Finally, the retail market is being expanded through the attempt of several publishers to reach other nonbookstore outlets for specialized works.

RESEARCH AND ADVERTISING

Some basic market research and analysis could help answer many questions to enable publishers and booksellers to create and market their products more effectively. But far too little has been done in this area. Few publishers have ongoing research departments. It is an area where a little well-spent money can produce profitable returns. Furthermore, much of the work could appropriately be done by the associations, as was the intent of the publishers and the ABA to cooperate in monitoring the impact of the "A Book Is a Loving Gift" advertising campaign in 1976 and 1977.

The economics of publishing make it difficult for the budget of any given title to provide much in the way of consumer advertising – nor has the effectiveness of advertising been measured in many studies. A publisher cannot do much to instill a brand loyalty for his house's products with the consumer, though the image of the imprint does carry some weight with retailers and authors. Publishers, and to a lesser extent some booksellers, have been getting bolder in trying new methods of reaching beyond their usual closely knit buyers market, trying television, radio, newspaper ads in nonbook sections, and mass transit posters. Bantam even tried pushing a popular title through a "trailer" in the movie houses. Although it was not convinced of its effectiveness, promoting mass market books at the time of showing a tied-in film is intuitively sound and is the type of innovation that must be tested in the search for efficient techniques to reach new potential purchasers.

The book clubs and mail order publishers have become most sophisticated in this regard, as they refine the process of mass mailings to a science, but similar advances still await the rest of the industry.

CONCLUSIONS

This study began with four hypotheses. The findings herein confirm most of them.

1.   Distribution problems are inherent in any industry with so much product. Cutting down the number of new issues will not solve the problem, merely ease one aspect of it, at the expense of a real solution. But the situation can be improved and made more efficient through the use of jobbers and wholesalers, with only modifications of the existing methods of operations for publishers. The methods and mechanisms for handling special orders exist as well.

2.   Access to books is becoming easier as the distribution of bookstores becomes more widespread and books are carried in a greater variety of outlets. But the process works both ways. The number of outlets will expand as the industry broadens the population of people who are interested in purchasing books. Conversely, the number of books sold will rise as books become available to a larger percentage of the population. That is, there is evidence that there is a large number of nonhabitual book buyers who will buy books if they are readily available from sources other than bookstores: chain retail stores, mail offerings, as premiums, and in retail stores selling specialized books as an adjunct to another product, such as cameras, hobbies, or plants.

3.   There is a strong sense of the need for sound business practices — a need that is coming from within the publishing world. A large measure of this is no doubt an outcome of the publicly owned houses having to be more responsive to their stockholders. In other cases, the wave of buying that brought

houses such as Random House into RCA; Holt, Rinehart & Winston and Fawcett to CBS; Little, Brown to Time Inc.; Quadrangle to the New York Times; New American Library into Times Mirror, etc., has made publishing executives more sensitive than ever to the bottom line. The rapid escalation in costs has also forced a re-evaluation of certain business assumptions, especially on the number of new titles to issue. But problems of marketing and distribution are still more acknowledged than acted on, with most change coming merely from individual efforts of various publishers to improve their own internal operations, within the context of the existing priorities. Though associations can recommend different distribution structures, e.g., more use of intermediaries, individual publishers must still decide if it is in their interest to change.

4. Both mass market paperbacks and the large-size trade paperbound books have been instrumental in keeping books an affordable commodity. As trade hardcover books advanced past the $10 market, the $2.25 or $3.95 paperbacks begin to look all the more attractive. The paper format and its accessibility to mass outlets will likely become the primary avenue for new fiction, as consumers continue to resist having to pay $6.95 or more for a work of an unknown novelist. Original fiction in mass market paperback has long been the province of the category books: westerns, mysteries, romances. The same will now be true for non-category fiction, providing the new author with exposure at $1.25. The booming business in remainders and reprints must be accepted by publishers as a clue to what can be done by pricing books at bargain prices and recovering costs by working on a smaller margin and a vastly greater volume. Not all books are appropriate for this path, however.

The proliferation of formats has both blurred the distinctions between categories of books as well as created new realities regarding subsidiary rights of titles. No longer does the hardcover publisher initiate all the projects or hold all the cards. Joint publishing ventures for many types of books will become more frequent, with multiple variations: in some cases mass market paper houses acquire all rights, spinning off hardcover rights and introducing the paperback version later, in the traditional way. In other cases, there will be simultaneous release of hardcover and mass market paperbook version, recognizing the perceived mutually exclusive markets for these. Trade paperback editions, moreover, become a third alternative, the rights to which may have to be negotiated separately. This format has barely been used for current bestsellers, but there is a feeling that it has vast potential to stake out a separate niche. The experience of Avon, Bantam, and Book-of-the-Month Club should provide some early signs of direction.

With it all, few doubt that the hardcover general book will be around well into the future. Not only does the library market demand the more lasting binding, but there is a hard core of bibliophiles who insist that a book is for keeps and who want the cloth-covered boards. Moreover, with the large-size paperbacks able to use the same printing plates and press runs, the process of putting hardcovers on a percentage of the copies makes the two compatible and ensures the economic survival of hardcovers.

Some structural changes among publishers have been taking place because of the new realities of the business. Hardcover trade houses are expanding horizontally in purchasing mass market paper expertise (e.g., Random House and Ballantine). Meanwhile, paperback publishers have found a synergy in having a trade affiliation, hence Dell's founding of Delacorte and its subsequent acquisition by Doubleday. The addition of separate trade paperback divisions, hardcover reprint imprints, or educational units is a natural extension of this movement.

PROSPECTS FOR THE 1980s

For the book publishing industry as a whole, the remainder of the decade will contain few surprises. The overall growth of publishers' sales will be largely a function of continued educational trends as well as the dynamics of general economic conditions, primarily inflation. It is unlikely, however, that the costs and prices of books will escalate at the rate of the 1973-1975 period.

Publishers' book sales by 1980 are predicted to be $5.8 billion, although a reasonable range could be between $5.4 and $6.4 billion. General books have been claiming an ever growing share of the total market, even during the educational boom of the 1960s. There is nothing to indicate that this trend should stop in the near term. College and el-hi textbooks will not be increasing their share, but general books may be finding expanding markets in the schools and colleges. Professional training and further specialization suggest continued growth in these high priced, low volume titles, whereas the increased acceptance of softbound formats for both trade and mass market bodes well for strong gains by both of these categories. Among general books, only religious and university press publishers can look forward to a flat or declining share.

The most unknown variable is the effect that an improved distribution network might have on book sales (as opposed to profitability). However, given the rate of change in the industry, the evolution of a reliable jobber system on a widespread basis would only begin to have a measurable impact by the early 1980s, so that such potential efficiencies have not been factored into estimates of 1980 sales.

FINAL WORD

There is a feeling of renewed energy and vitality afoot in the book world, a bit paradoxical in light of the leveling off of library expansion and funding, and the slowing down of the growth in the schools and colleges. What exists to compensate for these trends is the internal change that is underway in the industry in the distribution and marketing of books. Individual books may have to be sold, but a "book" is a presold concept in a highly educated society. No one must be told what a book is, how it works, or why it exists. With the addition of a few more leaders to the small vanguard now working to modernize a tradition-bound trade, book publishers can achieve an expanded role in education and entertainment, moving off the treadmill to currently unrealized growth. The key is improved distribution, in addition to selective but greater advertising and market research.

XIV

Profiles of Selected Companies

BAKER & TAYLOR COMPANIES
(Subsidiary of W.R. Grace & Co.)
151 Broadway
New York, NY 10036
(212) 764-7499

Baker & Taylor is the country's largest book jobber, with estimated sales of over $175 million. It is part of the giant W.R. Grace & Co. conglomerate, lumped into a consumer services division with Grace's 109-unit restaurant and 1752-unit catering facilities in the United States and Europe.

B&T is primarily a library jobber, fulfilling orders and processing books for 40,000 customers. It has five massive warehouses around the country, with anywhere from 110,000 to 130,000 titles in stock at any time, only 3500 of which are mass market paperbacks. Although Baker & Taylor retreated into the library jobber specialty after many years in the retailer wholesale business because it believed that this was the more profitable course, it has now embarked on a major re-entry into the retailer market. This will be a massive undertaking, since B&T's current systems are designed to process efficiently library orders calling for only one or two copies each of many separate titles. To sell to retailers, B&T will not only have to institute new procedures but even the layout of its warehouses may have to be changed. On the other hand, its huge inventories and current systems are well suited for handling special orders from booksellers.

Several other jobbers have run into serious financial trouble in recent years (Chapter VI) and W.R. Grace, surveying the book business, has apparently concluded that B&T is well placed to dominate the wholesaling and distribution field.

BANTAM BOOKS INC.
(Subsidiary of Bertelsmann)
666 Fifth Avenue
New York, NY 10019
(212) 765-6500

Bantam was established in 1945, with Grosset & Dunlap and Curtis Publishing Company as the major shareholders. In the mid-1960s, Grosset became the sole owner and in 1968 it, with Bantam, was purchased by National General Corporation, which in turn was acquired by American Financial Corporation in 1971. Three years later, Bantam was spun off to Italy's IFI International, which then sold a 51% interest in Bantam to Germany's Bertelsmann Publishing Group in 1977 for $43 million.

Through it all, Bantam has maintained its position as the leading mass market paperback publisher in the United States, holding a 22% or 23% share of the market. It has kept its leadership by carefully choosing editorial product and through its approach to distribution which is based in conservative print orders and the elimination of force-feeding its new titles to independent distributors.

Bantam's own record high for reprint rights was its $1.8 million bid for E.L. Doctorow's *Ragtime* (a disappointing performer as it turned out). It has published much of Solzhenitsyn's work and for many years published the highly acclaimed paperback literary review, *American Review*. Although well-known for the big titles — *The Exorcist, Jaws, The Deep, Trinity* — much of Bantam's profitability rests on its solid backlist and category fiction, including the westerns of Louis L'Amour or the romance novels of Barbara Cortland.

It was Bantam that pioneered the "instant" books, starting with the Warren Commission Report that was on the newsstands 80 hours after the report was made public.

Bantam has been in the forefront of the movement to use paperbacks in schools since 1958 when it began the Bantam Classics series. In 1963 it initiated its Pathfinder Editions, of which there are over 60 million in print. Skylark Books, a high quality line of reprints for children, was added in 1976. The Learning Ventures Division, also started in 1976, creates and markets multimedia programs, teachers' guides, and other educational packages directly to elementary and high school teachers.

Bantam continues to expand its educational sales, with almost 10% of total sales in the elementary and high school markets in 1966. Total revenues in 1976 were an estimated $85 million and 1977 revenue should have been between $90 and $95 million.

The publisher is giving greater attention to paperback original titles and has lead the way in seeking out first rights and then licensing hard cover rights out before publishing its own edition. Such was the case with Tom Robbins' popular *Even Cowgirls Get the Blues*. This way Bantam controls the terms and does not have to engage in bidding wars to such titles.

With an experienced and savy management team, Bantam has continued to thrive under a variety of owners. The company still has potential to expand its export sales, as well as its business through Bantam Books of Canada and its British subsidiary, Transworld Publishers, Ltd.

BOOK-OF-THE-MONTH CLUB, INC.
(Subsidiary of Time Inc.)
280 Park Avenue
New York, NY 10017
(212) 867-4300

Clubs:
> Book-of-the Month Club
> Cooking & Crafts Club
> Dolphin Book Club
> Fine Arts 260
> Fortune Book Club
> Sports Illustrated Book Club
> Quality Paperback Book Service

Book-of-the-Month is the prototype of book clubs, having been the first. Of the two major general interest clubs, it is generally considered that BOMC is the slightly more quality-oriented and the more conservative in its operations. There has been little growth in the membership of BOMC in recent years, although this is reported to be part of a strategy to replace poor members with a more "quality" (read "buy more books") membership.

In selecting each main offering, BOMC still relies on a very literate board of judges, so picks are presumably based on merit as well as marketability. However, management can still choose any other title as an "alternate" as it sees titles that it believes have a salable future.

BOMC is a financially sound corporation. Long term liabilities are limited to a lease and there are no outstanding notes. In short, this attractive, cash-rich posture made BOMC ripe for a takeover bid, and Time Inc. moved in with a take-over in 1977.

The main club has had to carry the burden of growth, accounting for 88% of company sales and 79% of its overall membership. The two book clubs from Time Inc., Fortune and Sports Illustrated, had been run under a strange arrangement, but in effect they were Book-of-the-Month Club operations with a royalty paid to Time Inc. for the use of the names. Although the Sports Illustrated Club has achieved a modest success, the Fortune club has had its troubles in acquiring members — even through *Fortune's* own mailing lists.

Much of the future growth of the company is riding on the success of the Quality Paperback Book Service, a bold experiment to expand the market for trade paperbound books. The growth of this operation has been slower than had been anticipated, but its membership finally reached 100,000 in 1977. The big problem that the QPBS has faced thus far has been in obtaining the paperback rights to good titles: most of its offerings consist of classical and literary backlist titles. Trade paper versions of *All the President's Men* and *Fear of Flying* were negotiated by BOMC solely for club use and much of the success of the club will depend on its ability in the future to get more publishers to sell these rights separately from mass market paperback rights. BOMC executives view the QPBS operation as a potential "historic force" and the "first genuinely new thing [in the industry] since the mass market paperback."

B. DALTON
(Subsidiary of Dayton Hudson)
Minneapolis, MN 55402

B. Dalton and Pickwick bookstores are subsidiaries of the giant Dayton Hudson Corp. retailing conglomerate that includes Lechmere in Massachusetts, Hudson's, Dayton's, and Target stores in the Midwest, and quality jewelry stores such as J.E. Caldwell in Philadelphia. Dalton is second only to Waldenbooks in total outlets with about 300 at last count, most of which are suburban mall locations. The average Dalton store has a healthy 30,000 titles and takes special orders. Sales in 1977 were about $135 million, accounting for an estimated 9% of all retail bookstore sales.

Dalton's stores range in size from 1500 to 10,000 square feet and generate anywhere from $70 to $125 per square feet in annual revenue. Dalton has eschewed any set formulas for location, looking instead for a favorable melding of educational level, transportation, income level, and absolute population in a given trading area. Similarly, it does not have set proportions for trade and mass market paperbacks, though the chain is primarily hardcover oriented. B. Dalton's does stock remainders at most locations. Recently, it has been following the industry trend of backing off from hardcover fiction because it just is not selling.

All book buying and reordering is done from corporate headquarters, except that a fast selling bestseller or a hot regional book can be ordered by the local managers (all salaried employees) from local wholesalers. There is no central warehousing, which led to the temporary dispute with Doubleday over Dalton's and Waldenbook's insistence on buying at 46% discounts, yet having books drop shipped to each individual store. (See Chapter IX.) Sales from each store are monitored through weekly and monthly store reports by titles and monthly analysis by categories. Since Dalton's major investment is inventory, control is a priority item and an area that management agrees is "difficult."

Dalton still does not advertise much on television and uses newspaper insertions in only a dozen markets. The major promotion is a yearly catalogue. Indeed, B. Dalton's spends less on advertising than the average retailer's percentage of sales, with total major market expenditure in newspapers in 1974 just short of $92,000 (which was likely matched with as much as $276,000 in cooperative funds).

The company seeks managers who enjoy the book field and manifest a desire to serve customers. A high percentage of managers are women. The managers are paid a base salary, plus an incentive based on merchandising and management controls. For example, window displays are considered a major input in manager evaluation. The company's stores are grouped into several regions, each under the supervision of a regional manager. Within the book world, Dalton's is generally rated as one of the better chain operations, primarily because of the depth of stock and traditional services it offers.

DOUBLEDAY & CO.
245 Park Avenue
New York, NY 10017
(212) 953-4561

Doubleday defines itself as a communications corporation. It is undoubtedly one of the most successful publishing companies in the United States, with extensive interests in publishing, printing, book clubs, book stores, and advertising. In fact, it is one of the few U.S. publishers that has total vertical capability. It can print, publish, promote, and sell a book all under one roof. The flagship of the company is Doubleday Publishing Company, which published 583 titles in 1976, mainly books designed for the general market: fiction, mystery, western, science fiction, nonfiction, juveniles, and religious books, including the prestigious Anchor and Image lines.

Doubleday entered the mass market paperback field when it acquired Dell Publishing Co. for $35 million in 1976. Dell specialized in paperbacks. Dial Books is a subsidiary. Doubleday's educational subsidiary is Laidlaw Brothers, a solid performer, and its reference book division is J.G. Ferguson Publishing Company.

Its distribution operations are the Literary Guild, the largest book club in the United States in terms of membership, and Doubleday Book Shops. Besides owning Feffer & Simons, one of the three largest U.S. export representatives, Doubleday's holdings abroad include Aldus Books in London, book club operations in Great Britain, Australia, and other English-speaking countries, and Doubleday Canada Ltd. Doubleday also has interests in broadcasting and advertising.

Doubleday had a record year in 1977, with sales of $336 million. The phenomenal sales of *Roots, Blood and Money, Trinity* and *Adolf Hitler* certainly helped. The Literary Guild increased its lead over Book-of-the-Month Club by a wide margin to become the largest book club in the U.S. Laidlaw Brothers had another successful year and Doubleday Book Shops and J.G. Ferguson Company returned to the profit column in fiscal 1977 after money-losing years. Dell suffered a marginal loss but did not affect the general profitability of the publishing division. Doubleday's overseas experience has also been excellent, with its book club operations abroad turning out to be winners.

HARCOURT BRACE JOVANOVICH, INC.
757 Third Avenue
New York, NY 10017
(212) 754-3100

Divisions:

- University and Scholarly Publishing Group.
- Periodicals and Insurance Group.
- School Materials and Assessment.
- Business Publications and Broadcasting Group.
- Financial and Popular Enterprises Group. (Sea World, Inc. is hub of group)
- Independent Publishing Units

>General Books Department
>Harcourt Brace Jovanovich Bookstore
>Editions Reconnaissance du Québec Limitée
>Editions Etudes Vivantes Limitée

During 1976 Harcourt Brace Jovanovich (HBJ) published 139 scholarly journals, seven magazines for farmers and stockmen,

Instructor for teachers, 645 school textbooks and related materials, 688 scientific and technical books, 233 college instructional works, 68 medical books, 61 business periodicals, 98 works in guidance and testing, 78 legal works, 13 newsletters, 107 hardcover books of belles-lettres, and 288 paperbacks.

Three categories of business constitute the bulk of HBJ's sales:

1. School Instructional Materials. In 1939 the firm's textbook business overtook the trade books and is now the major profit center of the company. Elementary school textbooks came into the company when HBJ merged with the older but smaller World Book Company, founded in 1905. In the elementary textbook field HBJ publishes in the subjects of reading, English, spelling, mathematics, humanities, social science, health, and science. The junior and senior high school textbooks are principally in the fields of English, science, social science, mathematics, business, and foreign languages. The majority of the school department's programs are prepared by the Center for Curriculum Development while the Center for Special Studies in Chicago develops new curriculums in language arts and social science for secondary schools. The Center for the Study of Instruction in San Francisco prepares elementary programs in humanities, social science, mathematics, music, art, and reading. The Division of Urban Education, also in San Francisco, publishes in the field of health education and compensatory education. The Instructor Curriculum Materials division of The Instructor Publications, Inc., produces teaching aids for the classroom. HBJ's more active school textbooks and related materials are revised every two to six years.

2. College Professional Books and Journals. The college department publishes college and university textbooks in the humanities, the social sciences, the natural and physical sciences, business, economics, education, and mathematics. Media Systems Corporation publishes materials for individualized instruction in community colleges and technical institutes and functions as a division of the college department. Academic Press, Inc. is one of the three largest scientific publishers in the United States. It publishes books and journals in the natural, physical, and behavioral sciences. It has an annual output of more than 500 books and 135 journals. Many of the journals are sponsored by scien-

tific and learned societies. Johnson Reprint Corporation publishes reprint and facsimile editions of rare or out-of-print materials, the most notable of which is the *Codex Atlanticus*, priced at $10,000 for a 12-volume set. Grune & Stratton, Inc. publishes books and journals in the medical sciences and in the field of special education including learning disabilities. Grune & Stratton and Johnson Reprint Corporation function within the Academic Press but retain their separate editorial and corporate identities. Harcourt Brace Jovanovich Legal and Professional Publications, Inc. publishes books and presents training programs in law-related fields. This subsidiary has its own printing and distribution divisions: Gilbert Law Printing and Law Distributors.

3. General Books Department. The general books department, including Jove Publications, Inc. (formerly Pyramid Publications), publishes about 370 new hardbound and paperbound books of adult interest each year. It also publishes each year about 30 hardbound juvenile books. The trade paperback list encompasses about 80 new adult and juvenile titles each year including original works and reprints. This department also publishes magazines under the Pyramid imprint. The books and magazines are distributed to the trade by Hearst Corporation and Curtis Publishing Company. Longman Canada Limited is a Toronto-based Canadian publisher of which HBJ is the majority shareholder and the Longman Group Limited, London, the minority shareholder.

HARPER & ROW
10 East 53 Street
New York, NY 10022
(212) 593-7000

Lines of Business:

- School Department (1977 sales: $15 million)
- Higher Education Group (1977 sales: $34 million). The group includes Dodd, Mead college titles acquired in 1975, Canfield Press, medical books, loose-leaf services, and journals, Harper's College Press, and the Media Department.
- Junior Books Department (1977 sales: $10 million)
- Religious Books Department (1977 sales: $4 million)

- Trade Group (1977 sales: $26 million)
- Basic Books, Inc. (1977 sales: $4.5 million)
- International Division (1977 sales $5.5 million)

Subsidiaries:

- Thomas Y. Crowell Company, Inc. (acquired in 1977)
- Conklin Book Center, Inc.
- Barnes & Noble Books

The main events in Harper's recent history have been the acquisition of Thomas Y. Crowell in 1977 and the agreement to acquire J.B. Lippincott, which took place in early 1978, when Lippincott shareholders gave their approval. Harper's expansion is all the more surprising because it began fiscal 1976 with a dismal drop in revenues in trade and junior books. In trade, Harper had no bestsellers for an entire year. However, it was helped by the good performance of its school and college departments. Gradually the overall picture improved. Trade books benefited from two bestsellers: *Thorn Birds* and *Oliver's Story*. Overall, revenues increased from $89.6 million in 1976 to $93.2 million in 1977, a gain of 4.1%.

The Religious Books Department at Harper became a free-standing publishing unit of its own by its move from New York to San Francisco. Another highlight was the signing of Betty and Gerald Ford to write their memoirs for publication under a joint Reader's Digest-Harper imprint.

In 1976, Harper & Row's largest stockholder, the Minneapolis Star and Tribune Co., increased its ownership to 38.6% of total shares.

INGRAM BOOK CO.
Subsidiary of Ingram Corp.
347 Redwood Drive
Nashville, TN 37217
(615) 889-3000

Ingram has helped bring book wholesaling out of the Dark Ages with the application of widely available technology (see the description in Chapter V). Ingram is part of a closely held conglomerate, the New Orleans-based Ingram Corp., with interests in construction, barge lines, and oil refining. Ingram was just another regional distributor when Harry Hoffman, former micro-fiche reader salesman for Bell & Howell, was brought in with dramatic results. Between 1971 and 1977, its sales increased from $5 million to an estimated $70 million, due in part to its acquisition of West Coast jobber, Raymar.

As part of a private company, Ingram is able to move fast — and it is willing to do so. With its goal of having a distribution facility within 300 miles of any retailer in the country, Ingram opened its first satellite warehouse in Jessup, Maryland, in 1975, finding a location, stocking the facility, and developing the operational procedures within weeks of making the decision to undertake the expansion move.

The challenge for Ingram still must be to increase its inventory. Currently it stocks only 18,000 titles for the microfiche system, although it carries an additional 45,000 titles as part of its library jobber business. Ingram feels that it can stock 80% to 90% of volumes requested with 20,000 titles. The Jessup warehouse started out with only 8000 titles, though that expanded in time. Ingram is very cost conscious, limiting toll-free calls to orders for a minimum of 50 books and requiring that such orders include Ingram's own title code for each book. Returns of trade books are limited to 10% of purchases (but there is no such limit on mass market paperbacks. The microfiche subscription program is actually a profit center for the firm, justifying its own sales force. With over 1800 customers, it is producing revenue exceeding $200,000.

As a national jobber, Ingram ranks second to giant Baker & Taylor. It is probably number one now in the retail trade.

CHARLES LEVY CIRCULATING CO./
COMPUTER BOOK SERVICE, INC.
1200 North Branch Street
Chicago, IL 60622
(312) MI2-4000

Charles Levy Circulating Co. is Chicago's primary independent distributor and the largest of its type in the country. Through its expansion as a national jobber with the Computer Book Service (CBS), Levy accounted for nearly 5% of the sales of mass market paperback books in 1975. Though there are economies of scale that make the extensive and sophisticated computer system feasible for the combined Levy/CBS operation, the firm cannot yet report that the expanded book operation is profitable.

The Computer Book Service has made impressive sales gains as the result of a campaign to recruit the country's largest chain store accounts. CBS's largest customer is J.C. Penney, but Sears has recently bought the CBS program. Kresge and Korvettes are among other major chain customers.

Using computer generated reports, the CBS system provides each store with a subsystem for ordering, inventory control, and sales reporting information. For the chain stores, it provides rack modules, four- or five-foot wide units, allowing expansion up to 40 to 50 feet of display area. CBS provides the initial inventory, along with optical scanning cards for each title. The program includes information on where each book should be displayed. The starting inventory is roughly tailored to the location of the particular store by producing a category breakdown for the new store based on sales by category of similar existing branches in the chain. From then on, new titles are sent automatically, as appropriate for that location. Reorders simply require department managers to pull the optical scanning card from the pocket when three copies remain of the title. Special orders are filled for a minimum of five copies per title.

In addition, CBS provides several reports:

• A quarterly activity register for each store in the chain. This summarizes sales by categories, including such information as returns and sales as percentage of shipments, allowing each store to adjust its product mix to maximize turnover.

• A category report by publisher, quarterly and year to date.

• The title comparison report, which provides a store-by-store analysis of the sales of eight titles, helping to find a pattern for bestsellers and to catch the peak sales period before the falloff.

- A hardcover breakdown by title and store, showing quantity and net dollars for each title, helping to make decisions on which titles to delete and which to add or expand at each location.

Internally, the Levy/CBS reports give net sales and returns by title, author, and category for each publisher and retailer, providing the company with highly useful information in its own book selection and allocation process. As a result, returns have decreased from 38% to about 32%, with a goal of 28%.

Besides this highly automated service, which is attractive primarily to chain stores that need such convenience, the system also allows the option of ordering from monthly new title announcements in advance of publication and monthly print-outs of the 6000 title inventory of paperback titles being warehoused. A WATS line is available to out-of-town customers.

Levy is quick to point to the dramatic results obtainable with its system. For example, up to 1974, the Walgreen Drug chain determined its own orders for its paperback racks. Then, Walgreen's turned over the book processing function at 130 of its 550 stores to Levy. In these stores, 1974 sales increased from $733,000 to $1,105,000, a 51% boost. Nor was this simply the result of expanded book departments, since sales per pocket jumped from $23.40 to $36.80.

Combining Levy and CBS sales, books now account for 40% of Levy's total volume. For local business alone, books are 26%, about average for large IDs.

MCGRAW-HILL BOOK AND EDUCATION SERVICES GROUP OF MCGRAW-HILL, INC.
1221 Avenue of the Americas
New York, NY 10020
(212) 997-1221

The McGraw-Hill Book Company publishes approximately 1700 new products every year. More than 80% of the Book Company's sales are to educational institutions and the remainder comes from professional, reference books, and trade books. The firm dominates in many areas of publishing including college and university publishing, business education, programmed reading, and technical, scientific, and industrial education. It also enjoys a modestly successful trade book program. Vocational education materials are published under the Gregg imprint, while Instructo produces supplemental educational materials for grades K-8. Educational Development Laboratories produces and markets innovative instrument-assisted programs. Other divisions are Professional and Reference Books, including professional book clubs; Schaum/ Paperback which publishes Schaum Outlines, Scholarly Books and Imports; Shepherd's Citations, which publishes citations, references, and indexes for the legal profession; and Webster, which serves the preschool through 12th grade with a full range of curricular materials.

Operating revenues for McGraw-Hill Book Company reached record levels in 1976 though earnings were lower than previous years. International sales rose 13.0% from $45.2 million to $51.1 million and domestic sales were paced by a hefty 39.0% gain in continuing education sales. The publicly owned company also benefited from the "back to basics" emphasis and a better than usual trade book season.

MACMILLAN, INC.
866 Third Avenue
New York, NY 10022
(212) 935-2000

Macmillan, Inc. is a diversified complex of autonomously operated companies. The principal book publishing division is Macmillan Publishing Company, Inc. Its School and College Divisions are the largest and most profitable components of Macmillan Publishing, which also includes The Free Press, Collier Books, Crowell-Collier Books, Threshold, and Hafner Press.

The other divisions include: Schirmer Books (music books); Glencoe Publishing Co., formerly Benziger, Bruce & Glencoe (The Benziger imprint specializes in instructional materials for preschool, elementary, and secondary schools; the Bruce imprint publishes textbooks for industrial arts; Glencoe Press specializes in textbooks for junior and community colleges); Berlitz Publications, Inc. (language instruction materials); P.J. Kenedy & Sons (publishes The Official Catholic Directory and other Catholic books); and Cassell & Company, Ltd. (British subsidiary, acquired in 1969, publishes general books, textbooks, and reference works).

Cassell & Collier Macmillan Publishers, Ltd., also based in the United Kingdom, has three units: Bailliére Tindall, publisher of professional books in the medical and veterinary fields; Geoffrey Chapman, publisher of religious and secular books, with emphasis on Africa, and Studio Vista, publisher of professional and general books in the graphic arts and architecture.

Other units are: Collier Macmillan International, Inc.; Editions Berlitz, based in Switzerland; Macmillan Educational Corporation, which produces all of the company's major reference works, including the Collier's Encyclopedia and Merit Students Encyclopedia, Hagstrom Company, Inc., map makers; Johnston & Bacon, based in Edinburgh, Scotland, which publishes maps, touring guides, and atlases; Standard Rate and Data Service, Inc., including National Register Publishing Company, Inc.; and Macmillan Information, which packages and publishes specialized data in science and technology, library science, and education.

Finally, it owns bookstores, including Brentano's in the United States and Claude Gill Books in the United Kingdom, and Macmillan Book Clubs, Inc.

Macmillan, a publicly traded firm, has a diversified output. Major areas of strength are encyclopedias, reference works, school and college textbooks, scientific and professional books, music, language instruction materials, professional books for educators, maps, and books of general interest in hardcover and paperback. It also publishes indexes, data banks, and other information products.

The year 1976 was among the most successful years in the firm's history. Macmillan's two major lines of business, publishing and instruction, accounted for over one-half of its total sales and revenues and almost three-quarters of its operating profit. Publishing, the larger of the two, increased revenues by 8.5% to $187.2 million, and profit by 32.5% to $22.4 million.

RANDOM HOUSE
(Subsidiary of RCA)
201 East 50th Street
New York, NY 10022
(212) PL1-2600

Imprints:
    Trade:
        Random House
        Alfred A. Knopf
        Pantheon
        Vintage
    Mass market paperback;
        Ballantine

Random House was acquired by RCA, the broadcasting and sundry services conglomerate, in 1966. At the time, the publisher had sales of $32 million. Now its revenue is included in a division which encompasses Banquet frozen foods, a carpet company, and Cushman & Wakeman real estate.

Random House sales did outpace overall publishing industry growth in 1977. Total revenue for 1977 is estimated to be $135 million, maintaining Random House as the largest trade book publisher in the country. Trade and juvenile contribute some $55 million (including Knopf, Pantheon, and Vintage), education sales about $35 million and mass market paperbacks about $43 million.

Ballantine, the mass market paperback subsidiary acquired in 1972, has consolidated its warehousing operation with the parent company and is able to draw on the same sales force. However, Ballantine has been working under a conservative strategy to build up a strong backlist, eschewing the bidding wars for reprint rights except for occasional books.

Random House has started its own mail order operation and has been expanding its sales in the education market through the highly structured Random House Reading Program, which packages trade books into graded reading packages, complete with recommended reading levels and supplementary teacher material. Random House is probably the major publisher of juvenile books and is the fourth largest dictionary publisher, based largely on its success with the Random House Dictionary. Among its most successful trade books in 1977 were John LeCarre's *The Honorable Schoolboy*, Carl Sagan's *The Dragons of Eden*, and Alister Cook's *Six Men*. Random also claimed good public acceptance for the new one-volume $65 *Random House Encyclopaedia*. Ballantine's sales grew three times greater than the overall mass market industry, paced by *Star Wars* and *Elvis: What Happened?*

TIME-LIFE BOOKS
Division of Time Inc.
777 Duke Street
Alexandria, VA 22314
(703) 960-5000

Time Inc. is the largest print publishing company in the U.S., with 1977 revenues of $1.25 billion and net income of $90.5 million. The largest magazine publisher in the U.S., Time Inc. also has significant interests in forest products, television and film, business data and newspapers. It acquired Book-of-the-Month Club in 1977 and owns trade and college publisher Little, Brown.

Its Time-Life Books division was begun in 1961 and in a dozen years had grown to become one of the major publishers in the U.S., and by far the largest mail order publisher.

Most of Time-Life Books revenues are accounted for by sales of continuity series, in which the customer is sent one book in a series at a time, with no commitment to purchase succeeding volumes. Recent strongly selling series have included *The Old West* and the *Encyclopedia of Gardening*. This form of publishing is relatively capital intensive, requiring enormous editorial investments for the four-color volumes (as much as $250,000 per volume, before printing) as well as multi-million dollar outlays for mailings and space advertising. The subscriber lists and advertising pages of Time Inc. magazines are obviously a key ingredient to success. The division also publishes such one-shots as *Time-Life Book of Needlecraft* and the fabulously successful *Best of Life*, which sold more than 1 million copies at $19.95

Time-Life Books markets its publications in many countries around the world and in 1976 international revenues were 42% of the unit's sales. It sold 15.9 million books and records in the U.S.

and Canada and 7.7 million in the rest of the world.

Boston trade publisher Little, Brown, plus the New York Graphic Society, contributed more than $35 million in book revenues in 1977. The 1977 acquisition of Book-of-the-Month Club will make Time Inc. one of the three largest book publishers and distributors in the U.S., with total book revenues around $300 million.

UNITED NEWS CO., INC.
850 East Luzerne Street
Philadelphia, PA 19124
(215) GA5-2800

United News is the major independent distributor (wholesaler) of paperback books and magazines in the Philadelphia area. It also owns a separate transportation company that distributes books and magazines to smaller IDs in the region.

Although its percentage of revenue accounted for by books is slightly lower than for IDs on a national basis, United News has placed considerable emphasis on this area of its business, including one of the country's more aggressive programs to sell mass market paperbacks in the schools. United has a full-time educational director who handles nothing but school sales, such as bookmobile fairs and the innovative book review seminars, which actually bring authors to the schools for autograph parties and discussions. So far, management admits that this line of business has not been profitable, but it expects that it will be.

United News's computer system analyzes dealer outlets by category of sales, combining information accumulated by its in-house data-processing system with the personal contact of truck men and their experience with the types of magazines that sell at each dealer. Distribution is made both through book trucks and prepacks, the latter being the predominant mode. As a result of its analysis, United News has been able to cut down its returns to under 40%, compared to the 48% to 50% national average.

United News officials admit that the profit on books is not commensurate with the proportional share of revenue, since they work on only a 16% gross margin when selling to many retail customers, as opposed to the 20% margin which applies more universally to magazines. They note that the sales of mass market paperbacks have been falling off in unit terms, but revenues are up due to higher prices. Although the ID is pleased with the trend of publishers to allow the wholesaler more latitude in estimating his needs for his own market area, United still feels that it is at a disadvantage compared to jobbers who can pick what they want, since the ID is expected to take some of every title a publisher offers. Nonetheless, United's managers feel that they can compete with the jobbers because they are local, take phone orders, and can provide one-day delivery.

Significantly, top UN executives are not worried about a glut of titles, arguing that we "don't need a cutback in titles — but more space for the retailer." One favorable trend for them has been the expansion of the supermarket outlets.

United News also owns seven retail bookstores in suburban shopping malls called the Nook of Knowledge. It has found these valuable in gaining retail experience, the better to be able to sell other retailers. United also uses these stores to show other retailers how they can operate better. Although the stores started with just magazines and mass market paperbacks, they now carry some trade hardcover — but not remainders. They have also found that greeting cards are an effective traffic builder.

WALDEN BOOK CO.
(Subsidiary of Carter Hawley Hale)
Stamford, CT 06904
(203) 359-2300

Waldenbooks is part of the enterprise that also runs the Broadway department stores, Neiman-Marcus, Bergdorf Goodman, and the Sunset House mail order gadgets firm. Waldenbooks had about 400 stores at the end of 1977. The eventual goal is to settle in at 500 units, closing and opening stores at a rate of 10 to 20 a year. Sales for 1977 were about $146 million, staying just ahead of rival B. Dalton, with just over 9% of the retail book market.

The average bookstore carries only about 10,000 titles, but this has been increasing in light of management's belief that "We can't make a go of it by catering only to those readers who like bestsellers." Such sentiments notwithstanding, Walden has had to retreat on a goal announced in a *Business Week* article on February 9, 1974. At that time, its president suggested that the chain would stock any book for at least six weeks if it was reviewed by a major publication. Eighteen months later, Walden admitted that inventory pressures forced it to scrap the idea before it was ever implemented, although it is aiming for a 15% to 20% overall increase in number of titles carried.

Because of the widespread information on sales coming into the headquarter's computer, Walden has the capability to spot national book trends early and has used this to suggest topics for new books to publishers.

Walden got its start running leased book departments in department stores, but these only account for 7% of its total stores. It tends to open in suburban shopping malls, looking for centers with the strongest national and local chain stores. However, in anticipation of running out of prime shopping centers in the next few years, Walddnbooks is looking ahead toward moving back into the cities, with 40 to 50 downtown stores in the planning stage. Sales in these locations must approach a high $150 a square foot versus the $110 target in a suburban store.

Walden has gone into the remainder business in a big way, having opened a separate remainder operation that sells to other retailers as well. It is also moving into the reprint field, and created 15 titles of its own in 1974. Remainders make up about 25% of volume, but this has been flat since 1972.

Waldenbooks has been very aggressive in advertising (see Chapter X), leaning on publishers for every cent of cooperative money it can get. Besides newspapers, it has experimented with radio, television, and even magazines.

Sources and Recommended Reading

Books and Market Studies

Dessauer, John P. *Book Publishing: What It Is, What It Does*. New York and London: R.R. Bowker Co., 1974.

Dessauer, John P., Paul D. Doebler, and E. Wayne Nordberg. *Book Industry Trends, 1977*. Research Report No. 4. Darien, CT: Book Industry Study Group, Inc., 1977.

Duke, Judith S. *The Children's Literature Market, 1977-1982*. White Plains, NY: Knowledge Industry Publications, Inc., 1976.

Kurian, George, ed. *Worldwide Markets for English-Language Books*. White Plains, NY: Knowledge Industry Publications, Inc., 1978.

Quirk, Dantia. *The College Publishing Market, 1977-1982*. White Plains, NY: Knowledge Industry Publications, Inc., 1976.

Quirk, Dantia. *The El-Hi Market, 1978-1983*. White Plains, NY: Knowledge Industry Publications, Inc., 1977.

Vanier, Dinoo J. *Market Structure and the Business of Book Publishing*. New York: Pitman Publishing, 1973.

Periodicals

American Bookseller, New York, monthly magazine.

BP Report on the Business of Book Publishing, Knowledge Industry Publications, Inc., White Plains, NY, weekly newsletter.

Educational Marketer, Knowledge Industry Publications, White Plains, NY, semi-monthly newsletter.

Publishers Weekly, New York, weekly magazine.

Reference and Directories

Association of American Publishers, *Annual Statistics*, New York.

Book Publishers Directory. Detroit, MI: Gale Research Co., quarterly and annual.

Bowker Annual of Library and Book Trade Information. New York, NY: R.R. Bowker Co., annual.

Literary Market Place. New York and London: R.R. Bowker Co., annual.

Appendix A

KNOWLEDGE INDUSTRY PUBLICATIONS
BOOK BUYERS SURVEY

The survey of book buyers sampled 75 people who had just been observed by the surveyor purchasing one or more books. The interviews were made in five bookstores, chosen randomly from the Philadelphia Yellow Pages Directory, March, 1975. Bookstores were those listed under "Book Dealers – Retail" and excluded those which specialized in "adult," medical, law, or religious books. All interviews were held during April, 1975.

NB: In tables that follow, some columns may not add to 100% because of rounding.

1. Number of books purchased in past six months: 2066
   mean = 27.5
   median = 14

2. Number hardcover: 397   Number paperback: 1669
   19.2%   80.8%

3. Reasons for buying books:

	number of books	%
a) formal educational requirements	246	11.9
b) business or work	278	13.5
c) personal interest	1331	64.4
d) gift	166	8.0
e) other	5	0.2
f) no response	40	1.9
	2066	99.9

4. Outlets used to purchase books in past six months:

	number of times mentioned	% of sample using
a) bookstore selling mostly hardcover	34	45
b) bookstore selling mostly paperbacks	63	84
c) book department of department store	15	20
d) card shop, drugstore, newsstand, supermarket, or other store that sells books as a sideline	13	17
e) college bookstore	24	32
f) book club	5	7
g) mail order	3	4
h) other	7	9

5. Factors influencing purchasing books at a particular store:

	most important reason	%
a) services offered	6	8
b) selection available	32	43
c) convenience to home	12	16
d) convenience to work	18	24
e) price of the books	2	3
f) other	5	7
	75	101

6. Most important sources in learning about each of the particular book (s) just purchased:

	number	%
a) recommended by sales help	2	2
b) recommended by friend, associate, or relative	19	21
c) book review	10	11
d) advertisement	4	4
e) browsing	43	47
f) bought at request of someone	6	6
g) other	8	9
	92	100

7. Last completed grade in school or highest degree:

	number	%
8th or less	3	4
9th through 12th	22	29
some college or higher training	15	20
college degree or better	34	45
no response	1	1
	75	99

8. Age:

	number	%
under 18	6	8
18-25	22	29
26-34	17	22
35-54	22	29
55-64	6	8
65 and over	1	1
no response	1	1
	75	98

9. Combined annual dollar income for all members of the immediate family:

	number	%
a) under $7500	3	4
b) $7500-9999	9	12
c) $10,000-14,999	9	12
d) $15,000-19,999	16	21
e) $20,000-24,999	9	12
f) $25,000 and over	15	20
g) refuse to respond	14	19
	75	100

10. Sex and race:

	number	%
male	32	43
female	43	57
	75	100
white	65	87
nonwhite	10	13
	75	100

INDEX

229

About the Author

Ben Compaine is director of studies and monographs for Knowledge Industry Publications, Inc. and is adjunct associate professor of marketing at Pace University. After graduation from Dickinson College, he earned an M.B.A. from Harvard Business School and taught marketing and management for eight years while completing a Ph.D. in mass communications at Temple University. His other published studies have covered the daily newspaper industry and the consumer magazine business. Currently a resident of Bedford, New York, he remains an avid Philadelphia-phile.